The Best Worst Christmas Ever

"Reading and rereading this humorous, heartwarming collection of stories is sure to become a treasured holiday tradition."

Wendy Toliver
Author of Disney's Once Upon a Time *books:*
Red's Untold Tale *and* Regina Rising

"… a delightful anthology of Christmas adventures. With varied experiences… this book shares hours of stories to brighten your holiday season. Jump into the homes and hearths of each writer as they relate memorable holiday moments which bring joy and laughter to your own celebrations. One can't read these stories without being profoundly grateful for the gifts of the season."

Christy Monson
Award-winning author of Banished *and* Becoming Free

"A delightful collection of Christmas stories to which many of us will relate… entertaining, lighthearted, and funny. It is a great book for your coffee table over the festive season for family and visitors to enjoy."

Lynnette Slogrove
Berkshire, England

"Reading by the fireplace on a rainy chilly day, I could not put this memorable book down. I have always loved the warmth and joy Christmas brings to my family, especially the little ones. This book shares the love of parents wanting to make the Spirit of Christmas for their children no matter the circumstances, to the *oops* of life that makes us laugh. The stories brought warm, loving memories of my own Christmas experiences. The stories will bring joy, laughter, and a lump to your throat."

Judy DeLong
Eden, Utah

"Who has not felt stressed and overwhelmed during the Christmas season? This charming anthology might just be what the doctor prescribes. Whether you are reading about a weary traveler trying to make it to loved ones for the holiday, a reveler attempting to find the perfect tree or the most appealing Christmas ornament, an exhausted cook, resolving that this Christmas is for relaxing instead, the reader is sure to find a story to smile about. Curl up with this book and some hot chocolate, and experience the camaraderie across the pages with others who have been there. Leading up to Christmas, these stories will surely help you connect to fellow strugglers, who, amid all the turmoil and hullabaloo, manage to experience the true spirit... nevertheless."

Kati Gibson
Ogden, Utah

"I found these stories, penned by various authors from around the world, delightfully funny and brilliantly written. The stories are told from the heart, for all to read and enjoy as I did. I can't wait to share this book with family and friends."

Janet Batisti
Ogden, Utah

The Best Worst

Christmas Ever

*Sometimes our well-planned Christmas turns out
to be less than perfect...*

25 Delightful Holiday Stories

Compiled and published by

Drienie Hattingh

Compiled by: Drienie Hattingh
Published by: Drienie Hattingh
Edited by: Marley Gibson

Cover Art: Brenda Hattingh
Cover Design: Dimitria Van Leeuwen

Photography: Drienie Hattingh, Brenda Hattingh, Matt Toliver, Juli Robertson, Lizel Sillman, Penny Ogle, Lynda West Scott, Alex Montanez, Elsabe Botha, Marley Gibson, Lizel Sillman, Dimitria Van Leeuwen

Printed in the United States of America
1st Printing November 2017

Published by:

Cardinal Rules
——— PRESS ———

Gerard Hernandez, the bravest little boy who
believes in the magic of rainbows.

Table of Contents

Acknowledgements..1

Foreword..3
by Drienie Hattingh

Introduction...5
by Tom Isbell

Cancelling Christmas...11
by Drienie Hattingh

The Candy Cane Christmas Tree Farm..21
by Terry Clancy

The Christmas Thief...25
by Brenda Hattingh

The Greatest Most Fabulous Christmas Tree Ornament in the World..............31
by Doug Gibson

The Tree Toppers...39
by Barbara Emanuelson

Barbie Dolls for Christmas..51
by Cindy Clark

Christmas Fudge for Bismarck..55
by Erika De Wet

Rudolph Cookies and a Shiny Disco Shirt.......................................59
by Lizel Sillman

The Sunflower Hat..63
by Margaret Zeemer

Furry Escapades..69
by Deb Rockwell

Father Christmas Knows Where You Are..73
by Drienie Hattingh

The Used Christmas Presents 77
   by Celeste Canning
Pumba the Potbellied Piggy 91
   by Juli Robertson
Christmas Was a Bummer 97
   by Alex Montanez
Where's the Ham? 103
   by Penny Ogle
The Worst Christmas Presents Ever 109
   by Ilze Botha
Christmas Veggies and a Three-legged Table 115
   by Mikki Ashton
Our Most Memorable Christmas Ever 121
   by Elsabe Botha
The Unwanted Christmas Tree 127
   by Alecia Drake
We Wish You a Merry Keys-mas 131
   by Marley Gibson
The Blackened Turkey 143
   by Rebecca Ory Hernandez
Batteries Not Included 147
   by Elsabe Both
A Christmas Quandary 151
   by Erica Hattingh-Smith
A Fiery Christmas 155
   by Rebecca Hernandez
The Best Worst Christmas Ever 161
   by Lynda Scott 161
About the Authors 171

Acknowledgements

My utmost thanks and gratitude goes to the authors who contributed their funny, unconventional, sometimes hilarious and even nostalgic, Christmas experiences to this anthology:

Mikki Ashton, Ilse Botha, Elsabe Botha, Celeste Canning, Terry Clancy, Cindy Clark, Erika De Wet, Alecia Drake, Barbara Emanuelson, Doug Gibson, Marley Gibson, Rebecca Ory Hernandez, Brenda Hattingh, Erica Hattingh-Smith, Alex Montanez, Penny Ogle, Juli Robertson, Deb Rockwell, Lynda West Scott, Lizel Sillman, and Margaret Zeemer.

Thank you for sharing your wonderful funny memories of Christmas in this anthology.

My love to my wonderful husband, Johan, who is always there for me and my supportive, loving children, Eugene, Brenda, Yolandi, and our beloved grandsons, Simon and Tristan.

Thanks to my editor extraordinaire, Marley Gibson. She is not only an amazing editor but also have the knack to make stories better by tweaking it... she makes them shine.

I love the cover of this book. The beautiful artwork was done by the talented artist, Brenda Hattingh and Dimitria VanLeeuwen was the excellent graphic artist. Thank you both! It is the perfect cover for this book.

Kudos to Janet Batisti, Judy De Long, Kati Gibson, Christy Monson, Lynette Slogrove, and Wendy Toliver, for taking time from their busy schedules to read the stories and write a review.

My gratitude to Tom Isbell—brilliant professor, actor, and author—who took time from writing his next book in the best-selling *Prey* Series to read these stories and write the introduction. Tom, I am honored by your participation.

My love and gratitude to my dear forever friend, Wendy Toliver, who wrote the back copy. You always have my back, dear Wendy, in all circumstances.

Thanks to all the readers who purchased this book. I am sure these stories will enrich your own holiday season with fun and laughter.

Geseende Kersfees and a very Merry Christmas to all!

Drienie

Foreword

Drienie Hattingh

I envision readers reading the first story in this anthology, *Cancelling Christmas*, on December 1st and the final story, *The Worst Best Christmas Ever*, on Christmas day.

It will give you a smile a day until Christmas.

Authors contributed stories from all over the United States: Scottsdale, Arizona, Santa Cruz, California, Flowery Branch, Georgia, Gramercy, Louisiana, Long Island, New York, Albuquerque, New Mexico, Savannah, Georgia, Wilmington, North Carolina, Seattle, Washington, Ogden and Salt Lake City, Utah, as well as Cape Town, Craddock, Roodekrans, and Pretoria in South Africa, and Tauranga, New Zealand.

Yes, Christmas is not always perfect. We plan, organize, make lists in order to have the perfect Christmas, but things often go wrong… as it did in all these stories. When things happened to these authors, it seemed disastrous at the time, but years later, they looked back and realized it actually turned out to be pretty hilarious and even nostalgic and definitely is now part of their family history.

The authors gladly shared their memories with me and I am honored to publish it for your enjoyment in this little Christmas book.

Keep this delightful anthology on your coffee table during the season and read from it on cold winter's evenings in front of the fireplace, or, your favorite stories out loud to visitors. All of the sudden, everyone's Christmas will become much more fun... and you may just find everyone around you telling of their own Christmas mishaps.

This is the perfect stocking filler for everyone on your list—it will become a favorite book for families to read every year.

Introduction

Tom Isbell

Stories of Christmas captivate us. Whether it's O. Henry's ironic and heart-rending *The Gift of the Magi* or the tear-inducing story of Truman Capote's *A Christmas Memory*, or Dylan Thomas's attempt to remember whether it snowed for six days and six nights when he was twelve, or twelve days and twelve nights when he was six, there is something captivating about tales of Christmas.

Maybe it's because our memories of that holiday run so strong and a well-told story takes us back ten, twenty, *fifty* years to a time when things seemed simpler and the past was viewed, if not in sepia tones, at least face-to-face and without the filter of an electronic screen.

Maybe it's because our memories of Christmas are so powerful that all it takes is a little nudge and we are young again.

Or, maybe it's because as we read these stories, we find ourselves *in* them.

As we read about searching for the perfect tree and ornament-obsessed cats, about the time we almost "canceled Christmas" or the time we wore a sunflower hat or served deviled eggs to strangers, we see our own experiences— moments which make us cringe all these years

5

later and those moments that still make our hearts soar.

The beautifully wrought stories in this vibrant new collection add to the mystique of the holiday season. They remind us of our past and take us back to simpler times. They bring back memories blessed and humorous. Most of all, they convince us we don't dare ever "cancel Christmas" again. The experiences, like the people they remind us of, are far too precious.

 **Tom Isbell** lives in Duluth, Minnesota. He was a professional actor for ten years in New York and Los Angeles. Now a playwright and novelist, he is the author of *The Prey* trilogy: *The Prey, The Capture,* and *The Release,* published by HarperCollins. He is a Professor of Theatre at the University of Minnesota Duluth.

Chapter

1

Cancelling Christmas

Drienie Hattingh

December 1998
Woodbury, Minnesota

I stopped in the middle of the aisle of
Target's holiday section and whispered,
"What *am* I doing?"

My cart was loaded with stuff for Christmas.
New green and red glass balls to replace the old,
faded, and broken ones I have used since we
arrived in Woodbury, Minnesota, from South
Africa ten years before. There were also a couple
of cute, new ornaments and an updated string of
colorful lights for the tree so I didn't have to go
through the old string, checking every bulb,
looking for the one that caused the lights not to
work. Of course, no Christmas would be perfect
without a beautiful red poinsettia with bright

green leaves to set on our oak dining room table. This one was spectacular. I got the best one because I was here early.

I pointed my shopping trolley to the other part of the store where I would buy all the ingredients for cookies, pies, and Christmas Eve dinner with the works. But, I did not move. I simply stood in the Christmas section, staring at the basket and its contents, yet not really seeing it. It all blurred as my internal conversation continued.

Why am I doing this?

Who cares if I produce a perfect Christmas or not?

Our children wouldn't be home. Eugene was in Hawaii on military duty. Brenda was in New York, performing in a play right up until the 25th. Yolandi was in Duluth, happy to host her first-ever holiday celebration with her friends, in her new apartment.

Added to all of this—my husband, Johan, could not care less about the holiday. He has always complained about the preparations and presents and decorations for Christmas. Often, he's said he wished we could just go away at Christmas time.

Sometimes, I've agreed with Johan, thinking it would be nice to have a peaceful end to December and concentrate on the "real reason for the season." I've dreamt of having Christmas up north in Minnesota, in a snowed-in cabin in the woods, just the two of us. No fuss, no tired, sore feet and legs, and none of that having to take-Christmas-down.

I hated that part so much. Removing the ornaments off the tree, taking it down, pulling the wreath from the front door, and stowing it all away in the basement for another year.

Johan often mumbled, "It would definitely cost less if we had a peaceful Christmas. I wish we could just skip Christmas," he lamented.

I looked up, my eyes wide as if awakened from an unsettling dream. Through the holiday haze surrounding me, it was as if a light bulb shone in the distance.

"That is it. I am cancelling Christmas!"

I did not realize I'd uttered this out loud, but a woman who frantically rushed by me with an overflowing cart—with a pretty shabby-looking poinsettia perched on top—looked at me in shock. I lifted my chin in defiance.

I retraced my steps and put everything in my cart back where it belonged. I did hesitate when I reached for the stunning poinsettia. I'd spent at least fifteen minutes picking out the perfect one.

"No..." I whispered. "You can do this!"

And I did.

I put the beautiful potted plant back and noticed there were now much fewer poinsettias than when I'd picked mine about half an hour ago. As I put it down, a woman practically grabbed it at the same instant I pulled my hands away. A sickening feeling formed in my stomach.

I walked out of Target without buying anything. As if nature wanted to remind me what a terrible thing I was doing, it started to snow. Beautiful, big snowflakes drifted over me as I walked to my car.

That night, I surprised Johan with a lovely home-cooked meal.

"I thought you are starting to bake Christmas cookies tonight," he said with a frown.

"Nope," I said, not looking at him. "I decided not to do that this year."

"What?" He asked in utmost confusion. "Why not?"

"Well, the children are not coming home, so I decided not to do Christmas." I concentrated unnecessarily hard on placing the pork roast exactly in the middle of the table.

Johan laughed. "You are kidding, right? Look," he said, probably noticing my lower lip quivering and appearing a bit flustered, "I brought the tree in from the garage. I will put it up if you'll tell me where."

"That won't be necessary," I said, lifting my chin and smiling bravely. "You can put it back in the garage. Come on, the food is getting cold."

I started dishing up dinner and changed the conversation, telling him about how well Brenda's play was going and how happy Yolandi was in her new apartment.

Johan took the loaded plate I handed him and said, "Cancelling Christmas? Are you serious? Are you sure?"

"Yes," I said with a smile, "I am! It will be silly to do everything just for us. Besides, you aren't crazy about the holiday anyway. I mailed the children their presents and all."

"You're okay with this?" he asked with his eyes pulled in slits.

"Yes, I am," I told him. I've said it so many times by now I've started believing myself. "We can have the peaceful Christmas we have talked about… at last."

He regarded me and nodded his head. "I have to agree it would be silly to go to all that trouble with the children away. Besides you are always so exhausted afterward."

We finished our dinner and Johan helped me clear the dishes. He even made coffee.

A week passed where I did not know what to do with myself. Every house in the neighborhood was decorated with lights in the trees and wreaths on the front door. The one thing I did do, as I've done since we were married, was to put up the nativity scene. This, after all, was the reason for this season. I dabbed at tears as I put the precious porcelain nativity, in soft muted colors, Brenda had bought me, in its usual place on the coffee table in front of the window. Outside, the snow was softly coming down.

Johan surprised me one night when he returned from work with a Christmas wreath.

"We can at least have this," he said with a smile as he held up his find. He'd also brought us a pizza—my favorite, Hawaiian. We ate in front of the TV, watching the news with a lot of Christmas-related topics. We could not find a movie to watch because every single movie was season related.

My friends, whom I would often meet for lunch or coffee, weren't available because it was now a week before Christmas and they were all running around like crazy getting everything on their own lists done. I sat in my sitting room, reading and listening to Christmas music.

The children called every now and again, but I did not say anything about cancelling Christmas. They had received their gifts and were elated with what I bought them.

Two days before Christmas, very early in the morning, I was awakened by the phone. It was Brenda calling from New York.

"Mom!" she almost shouted in the phone. "I am coming home for Christmas. The director decided to end the show a couple days earlier. Attendance dwindled a lot and we all really wanted to be with our family for the holidays. So, I am catching a flight tomorrow afternoon. I'll be home Christmas Eve… I cannot believe it, can you? Oh, and I cannot wait to see our house all decked out with the lights on the tree out front and in the kitchen window… that is always so pretty. And your ginger and sugar cookies. The nativity scene. The Christmas tree… all of it. Is it snowing? I cannot wait to sit down to your amazing Christmas Eve dinner with all the fixings."

I was completely silent as she seemed to rattle off all of her requests and excitements in one full sentence. I was trying to wake up completely, think straight, and find my voice.

"Mom? Are you there? Can you hear me?" She paused for a moment and then asked, "Awww… are you crying."

I found my voice again and realized I *was* close to tears, but not exactly for the reasons Brenda thought.

"Oh, Brenda... that... is... so... so wonderful. I am... speechless... I..."

She interrupted. "Got to go, Mom. We need to break down the stage today. See you tomorrow."

The phone went dead.

Johan was already up and in the shower getting ready to leave for his last day at the office before the holiday... our supposedly peaceful one. Little did he know.

When he came into the room, he saw me sitting up in bed with the phone in my hand just staring at it.

"What's wrong? Who called?"

"Brenda's... coming home for Christmas."

Johan started laughing. "Oh, boy!"

Something I found out that day—that very day before Christmas Eve—was I'd spent too much time getting ready for Christmas in the past. That year, despite my edict not to do anything, I managed (with Johan's help) to do *everything* in one-and-a-half days.

He actually called his office and cancelled his appointments for that last day, which amazed me. He'd somehow received a huge dose of the Christmas spirit right when *I* needed it.

He retrieved the tree from the garage and immediately put it up. Then, he dragged the boxes of ornaments up the stairs and—I never thought I would ever see this—he decorated the tree while I started baking batches of Christmas cookies; all the ones I knew Brenda loved.

Through all that, I put up the Christmas village and threaded the fake pine strings around the banister leading up to the sitting room.

Glancing down at my watch, I told Johan I had to go to the store right then. I had to go now so I could spend tomorrow preparing everything for the Christmas Eve dinner and give the house final once-over, put clean sheets on Brenda's bed, and make sure her bathroom was clean.

Johan said, "Go, I'll do the rest."

As I headed for the door, he called out, "Just tell me where these go."

When I turned, I saw him pulling a mangled bunch of lights out of a box. I felt sorry for him.

"Everywhere! On the Christmas tree, inside the kitchen window, through the pine strings on the banister, and on the tree in the front garden. Good luck."

I was about to open the car door when I remembered my baking, "Please remove the cookies from the oven when the timer goes off and put the next tray in."

I told him this last bit not really believing he would actually do it. I couldn't imagine him taking over my Christmas baking. Johan was never in the kitchen, except to eat. However, desperate times called for desperate measures.

I drove as fast as the icy, snow-packed roads allowed with my original list in my purse.

Arriving at the store, I ignored one side of the list—the side with new glass balls, new ornaments and new strings of light. The old stuff we had would have to do. I aimed straight for the groceries and ticked items off as I went: ham, glaze, pineapple, potatoes for mash, sweet potatoes and marshmallows, green beans and fixings for the casserole...

I had to confess; I improvised.

I bought ready-made pecan and pumpkin pies, rolls, and the frozen whipped cream. No time to make those from scratch.

Remarkably, I found a poinsettia, one of two left on the almost-empty shelf, littered with dead leaves. I put it on top of the groceries and rushed through the checkout. Outside, it was snowing harder as I went slipping and sliding to my car, hanging onto the cart for dear life.

When I arrived home, it was dark and still snowing. I halted like a cartoon character in the circle in front of our house. The sight that greeted me was divine.

All of a sudden our house wasn't dark spot between our neighbors' houses anymore. The pretty scene before me brought tears to my eyes. The lights were twinkling in the kitchen window, in the tree out front, and from the wreath on the front door.

He did it… thank you, Johan.

As I walked into our house, I noticed two things: the sweet aroma of the last batch of ginger cookies and how everything was enveloped in the soft glow of the Christmas tree lights.

I put the poinsettia on the dining room table as Johan walked down the stairs.

"Ta-da!" he said with his handsome smile.

I ran into his arms and we hugged for a long time in the soft glow of the season.

He whispered in my ear, "We did it. Brenda won't suspect a thing."

Chapter

2

The Candy Cane Christmas Tree Farm
Terry Clancy

December 1984
Seattle, Washington

W hile I was growing up in Seattle, Washington, it had been a tradition in my family to purchase our Christmas tree the weekend of, or after, my birthday on December 8th. I continued the tradition after I got married.

When I was a child, I remember my dad piling us all into the car to go get our Christmas tree. We always lived in cities, so we would go to the local lot and search for the perfect tree. Mom was the one who picked the tree that called out to her.

When we got home, Dad sawed off the end of the tree and placed it in a bucket of water to hydrate while he untangled the multitude of strings of lights. He meticulously checked every bulb to make sure they worked. Once the tree was in the stand and put in place in the living room, Dad would start the Christmas music and Mom would get out the decorations. Dad's favorite decoration was the silver tinsel which he would put onto the tree one piece at a time.

My favorite memory is stories attached to each ornament which Mom and Dad would recite as all of us decorated the tree.

After I got married, we lived in Redmond, on the east side of Seattle. My husband, Chuck, and I would go up into the mountains and cut our tree at a Christmas tree lot named *The Candy Cane Christmas Tree Farm*. The farm was basically the owner's land he opened up to the public to cut trees themselves. There was a hut where we got our saw and a cup of hot chocolate. The kids could sit on Santa's lap while the parents pay for the tree.

I loved the smell from the freshly cut tree.

Like clockwork, it was always rainy and misty when we arrived.

The year, I was pregnant with our son, Ian. I told Chuck I wanted a tree bigger than me. The one we found ended up taking up almost a third of the living room. It was a Shasta. I have never found another one... loved that tree.

True to so many traditions, this one, too, was quite the chore. There were no manicured paths or trails. It was rough going up and down hills and we would come away with quite a few scratches from the trees which were sometimes quite close together. However, we loved it.

When our daughter, Maureen, was born, tree-cutting got even more involved and strenuous.

We would put her in the back carrier and hike all over the tree farm to get our perfect tree. It was not only hard work, but it was also a bit unpleasant because of the rain. Regardless, we prevailed. After all, nothing good can be gained without hardship... or so we seemed to believe... until Maureen got wise.

At first, she did not mind. She would sit all snug and warm on her dad's back, enjoying the outing and even dozing off now and again. When her brother, Ian, was born, things changed. She did not seem to care that much about tradition at all... or finding the perfect tree. Now, she had to walk because Ian was in the carrier. This was not to her liking at all. She was a smart girl.

One rainy December day, Chuck was busy strapping Ian into his carrier and I was getting my backpack with necessities on.

Maureen yelled, "This one."

Chuck and I looked at each other in surprise. Maureen had jumped out of the car and run to the first tree she saw, the closest to the car, and declared her choice.

Chuck and I laughed at her cuteness but of course, we could not allow this. We had our time-honored holiday traditions to consider. We were not city folk who went to a tree lot, pointed to the biggest, already-cut fir or pine and said, "That one please." And then, let the attendant wrap it and load it up on the roof.

No way.

Not us.

We *had* to spend hours looking for the perfect tree in a forest, saw it down, drag it to our car, and strap it onto the roof ourselves. This was a tradition and adventure and, by golly, come rain or mud, we would keep by it. We had to suffer through it all.

So, we would drag Maureen all over the farm for a couple hours, stopping time and again, admiring trees, judging the size and all.... up hills, down hills, and down gullies we would go.

Eventually, though, when we felt the time was right (and we had suffered enough) and listened to Maureen calling out again and again, "This one, this one," we stopped at the tree Maureen initially picked out, right next to our car, and took it home with us.

Chapter

3

The Christmas Thief

Brenda Hattingh

December 1992
Woodbury, Minnesota

hen I was a teenager, my parents gave me a cat for my birthday. Since he was orange colored, I called him Ginger. Yes, a boy cat named Ginger.

He was the kind of cat who turned cat haters into cat lovers. He was a spunky, quirky cat who loved to cuddle. He slept across my neck until he got too big and then would sleep nestled in the crook of my knees.

He did all the usual cat things like bringing us dead birds as a trophy, that my mom would discard in the trash to his dismay. But, it was the unusual things that made him the cat he was. Some of them presenting a mystery before the truth was revealed.

My mom called my brother, sister, and me into the kitchen one day and demanded to know who had been eating corn on the cob and tossing the bare cob on the floor. We all denied it vehemently, but she was not convinced.

It wasn't until a few days later when she was boiling corn again that someone noticed Ginger brazenly hopping up onto the counter and batting an ear of corn out of the boiling pot onto the kitchen floor with the flick of a paw. He then got down on the floor, placed a paw on one end and commenced to chew the corn all the way across, before rotating it for the next row, kind of like typing on an old typewriter and hitting the return handle.

The corn culprit had been found out, but the behavior was too endearing to punish.

Another one of his quirks was hiding around the corner at the top of the stairs. When I rounded it, he would jump up and bite my rear end. He only did this to me and seemed to find great joy in it. It got to the point where I was terrified to round that corner at the top the stairs.

Ginger was an indoor/outdoor cat and would sometimes disappear for up to three days at a time, only to return with a wounded ear from one of his neighborhood battles... (I'm convinced he won every one of those.) Once, I was driving home from school and saw him sitting on the corner of our block, surrounded by other cats, one of whom was rubbing up against him lovingly while he stared into the distant sunset. That was when I realized he was king of the cats in our neighborhood, a title I was sure he had definitely earned.

And so, it came to be one Christmas that a very strange phenomenon came about in our home. Ginger developed some sores on his chin. Being quite concerned, my mom took him to the vet immediately. There were several small punctures on his chin in varying stages of healing. Some were open wounds, some were scabbed over, and some were at a later stage of healing. The vet was baffled as to what the cause could be, but assured my mother the wounds were superficial and not a life-threatening illness. He sent Mom and Ginger home with some topical cream for the mysterious wounds and recommended we keep an eye on him.

Days went by with presents slowly piling up under the decorated Christmas tree and fresh snow piling up outside. Despite Ginger's tiny injuries, his spirits were high as ever. He was enjoying his corn on the cob and still jumping up to sink his teeth into my derrière whenever the opportunity presented itself—still the charming cat enticing visitors into snuggling with him on the couch. However, our concern grew as new wounds continued to appear while older ones scabbed over and healed.

Around this time, my mom noticed her small Styrofoam snowmen disappearing from the decorated Christmas tree. As with the corn on the cob incident, we three siblings were once again questioned. Again, we denied the accusations and had no idea where the snowmen might be hidden. Their white Styrofoam bodies decorated in red and green seemed to have vanished into thin air.

Christmas day was drawing closer and it was time to clean. My mother did her usual vacuuming, which included moving furniture to get behind the couches. It was upon one fateful afternoon when she discovered a pile of Styrofoam snowman behind the living room couch. When we arrived home from school, we were again questioned. We knew nothing, or as my mother thought, no one was talking. She simply hung the snowmen back in the tree.

The next day, the snowmen disappeared again. This time, she knew where to look. Lo and behold, there they were behind the couch. She questioned the three of us and was, again, met with our denial. She asked Dad if he was pulling some kind of prank, but he wasn't at fault, either.

Shortly after, my father left on a business trip. As usual, Mom made the rounds to make sure we were in bed and the doors were secured. She locked the front door to a quiet house when she walked up the stairs to the living room and stopped her dead in her tracks.

She couldn't believe her eyes.

In the light of the Christmas tree, Ginger stood up on his two back legs, masterfully balancing as he carefully stuck out his neck and grasped a Styrofoam snowman between his teeth. He barely flinched at the pine needles pricking his chin, creating fresh puncture wounds, before lowering his loot to the ground and running off to stash it behind the couch.

It was the corn thief, the derrière attacker, the king of the neighborhood cats, the master of it all, at work once again.

I often wondered what went on in his head. If he simply loved those snowmen so much or if he thought it would be so funny to fool us all into blaming each other for their disappearance. Maybe I'm giving him too much credit, or... maybe not.

My mom still has some of the Styrofoam snowmen with Ginger's teeth marks in them.

Though he passed away many moons ago, his legacy lives on and we still tell the stories of our cunning funny family member who stole our corn, our snowmen, and our hearts.

4

The Greatest Most Fabulous Christmas Tree Ornament in the World

Doug Gibson

December 1968
Long Beach, California

M y father found the greatest, most fabulous Christmas tree ornament in the world.

He loved arranging contests for us kids that captured his fancy for a week or so. If he saw a great track race on TV, the kids ran fifty-yard dashes. If a player snagged a baseball impressively, several still-to-be-coordinated children were at the park trying to make spectacular catches of balls lobbed by Dad.

This particular December, Dad's boredom with a quiet stay-cation pre-Christmas ceased when he saw a photo of a nineteenth-century Christmas tree in a magazine. It wasn't the tree he loved, rather it was the ornaments. They were all antique-looking with simple designs and delightfully intended sentiments.

After sharing the photo with the rest of us, the decree came: The family would search for the perfect Christmas tree ornament.

The kids, including Baby (our nickname for our eighteen-month-old brother), went to the Pic N Save to find an ornament. We were annually presented with a five dollar bill to buy presents and other holiday accessories. In those days, you could buy eight or nine kid-appropriate presents and still have twenty cents or so left over to buy an ornament.

Dad understood that Pic N Save or even Sears & Roebuck had limited ornament opportunities. He was more cunning. Accompanied by Mom, he headed to an antique store. It was there, in the holiday celebration section, he saw it.

The ornament was shaped like a bell, not too large. What had once been a light shade of red had aged to a dark pink color. A wrapped present adorned one side. Beside it, etched in tiny letters, were the words "Merry Christmas." On the back side, the glass of the ornament had diminished to where you could faintly see beyond the covering into the interior.

Likely no great shakes when it was created, it still had mystique several scores of years later, mostly because it was still there after so many years. Further developments would prove it should have remained on a shelf to be admired.

As Mom recalled, Dad clapped his hands and ran toward the ornament, catching his coat in the exterior of a box of old Christmas cards. He shook off his sleeve, ignored the scattered cards, and reached the ornament a split second before a lady who had sprinted from the toy department.

"It's mine!" she screeched to Dad. "You were in the Christmas cards. I called for this."

"I had it reserved! I had it reserved! I was in the Christmas area. You can reserve anything you want in the toy area, but I reserved this," Dad countered loudly.

"No, sir. It's mine."

The dispute continued on its way to the office of the antique store manager. He resolved it in Dad's favor in the time-honored profession of possession being nine-tenths of the law.

Dad gloated over his win in the great Christmas ornament contest. He merely smirked at the ornaments we'd purchased for a quarter (or under) made from yarn and such. There was a semi-approving nod toward the ugly, plastic ornament Baby had picked out that had "White Christmas" etched on one side.

Carefully holding the greatest ornament of all times between both of his thumbs and forefingers, Dad placed his prize near the top of our artificial white Christmas tree.

Mother, who loved Dad more often than she liked him, gave a perfunctory bow to the winning ornament, and then placed our decorations throughout the tree. She put Baby's just below the antique. Through it all, Dad beamed at his ornament, ignoring snippy comments from Mom about the "greatest, most fabulous, most expensive Christmas tree ornament ever."

Dad found it necessary to increase protection for the greatest ornament when Baby—who'd been hoisted up high by the assistance of a sibling accomplice—grabbed onto the winning ornament with chubby hands. As Baby began a tumble into the tree, little fingers slapped against the faux tree needles, causing a repercussion that sprang the greatest, most fabulous ornament into the air.

Dad bellowed out, stepping over Baby to catch the flying ornament. He caught it with a backhanded grab that would have made the California Angels' shortstop, Jim Fregosi, proud.

Holding the ornament in hands cupped together, he silently went into the kitchen.

When he returned, the greatest ornament sat in a single cradle created from an egg carton. Supporting the nestled and cradled ornament were eight Popsicle sticks; four at the sides and four supporting both ends. The cradle was clumsy and perhaps too large, but spread across three faux branches near the top of the tree, it was a reasonably secure fit.

Dad moved Baby's White Christmas ornament to a lower branch and declared the toddler grounded—literally—for the duration of the holiday season.

As Christmas drew closer, we got used to Dad's frequent verbal toasts to the greatest, most fabulous Christmas tree ornament ever and his condescending faint praise for our yarn balls which were no longer wound so tight.

We kids often allowed neighborhood cats into the house. They attacked the yarn bulbs.

That horrified Dad, being scared his precious antique ornament would break, so he did his best to keep the cats out. As a result, two of the yarn balls were connected by a thick string about eighteen inches long.

Oh yes, Dad also continuously decreed Baby's ornament choice as the runner-up, promising the delighted child the first taste of cookies on Christmas Eve.

On December 23rd, Dad and Mom invited some of their friends over for eggnog. Other than Dad's occasional mentions on the job or at church, these revelers had never seen the greatest ornament. They were impressed with the authentic aging and old-fashioned dignity of the ancient adornment. There was much praise, oohing, aahing, and wonderment over Dad sleuthing out such a find.

Dad, who rubbed his hands together in anticipation of the party and praise, tried hard to present a modest countenance, but failed badly. So intent was he with the long-awaited praise, he neglected to notice a tiny visitor as impressed as any adult in the room. The rest of us had stayed just outside the party, eating sweets in the kitchen. However, Baby simply had to touch the forbidden ornament.

An ill-fated idea to climb to the protected ornament ended quickly when Baby tripped over the connected, cat-maligned string ornaments. Chubby fists waving high above his head grasped at faux branches to no avail.

Baby fell forward; several branches snapped upward. One broke exactly under the egg carton cradle, lifting the greatest, most fabulous Christmas tree ornament high in the air outward, aimed toward the many presents gathered around the tree.

Wordlessly, Dad sprang into action. He only had time to make a shoestring catch an inch above the closest present, but he managed it as well as Willie Mays in the San Francisco outfield. Triumphantly, Dad turned, holding the ornament up for all to see. The front of the ornament was undamaged. Unfortunately, though, the back had Dad's pinky finger sticking through a large hole.

A collective gasp filled the air and everyone... waited... anticipating what would happen next.

Dad tried to remove his finger very slowly. Just as the final part of his appendage came out, the entire ornament collapsed within itself.

The gasps shifted to sighs, then silence.

The greatest, most fabulous Christmas tree ornament... was no more.

A long stillness followed.

For a moment, Dad's face resembled Marlon Brando's in *The Godfather* when learning of his eldest son's murder.

And then, a normal expression returned.

Dad picked up a whimpering Baby and plopped a kiss on the toddler's cheek. He reached for the White Christmas ornament and put it in Baby's hands. Together, they placed it into the makeshift cradle.

Dad smiled and announce, "Now, *this* is The Greatest, Most Fabulous Christmas Tree Ornament in the World."

Chapter 5

The Tree Toppers

Barbara Emanuelson

December 1969
Wilmington, North Carolina

N othing compares to decorating for Christmas.

When I was growing up, it was always a family event, complete with a blazing fire in the old-fashioned fireplace of our colonial-style home. Fragrant mulled spices filled the house with cinnamon, apples, and Harry Simeon's *Chorale* played in the background.

There was also my mother orchestrating everything.

My father didn't say much, even though we could see the dread on his face when my mother would declare, "Today's the day!"

This was the magical time in which our house was donned with the festive pinecones, wreaths, candles, and lights. All that glittered was gold. Literally, every ornament on our Christmas tree was gilded in color, playing off the shimmering lights. There might be a smattering of silver thrown in here and there or an occasional pop of red. My mother meant for our tree to represent opulence… so it did.

The year I was thirteen, we had kittens in the house at Christmas-time. The week before Halloween, my beautiful calico cat, Channie, gave birth to a litter of kittens. Her eight babies were a mix of calico, orange and white, and black and gray with tan spots.

My dad went to the store for a big moving box for our feline mama and her little ones. He cut a side out, but left the front and top opened so Channie could easily get in and out. He put in a nice, comfy foam cushion with a warm blanket on top of it so Mama and babies could sleep and nurse in luxury. The box was nestled in the corner of the dining room, opposite the coat closet.

By the time we began decorating for the holiday season, the kittens were six weeks old and had started to get rambunctious. It was my job to watch them and make sure they didn't get underfoot so Dad could remove the coats and open up the panel in the back of the closet to get to the storage area.

He put the coats on the dining room chairs.

"Don't let them anywhere near, Barbs," my father admonished, pointing at the kitties.

"Okay, Daddy," I said, even as the most spirited of the kittens, Coco, was escaping.

Channie was happy to sit outside the box and let me be the babysitter, something I often did so she could get a break from the mewing and hungry babies. This time, they were poking their heads out, trying to see what the excitement.

By the time Dad got everything out of the closet, the babies were beside themselves, squealing with curiosity and itching to see what the fuss was about.

"Get back in there, Coco. You, too, Tarzan. And you, Moonshine. Grrrrr... Can't I let them out?" I begged.

"Yes, Barbs. Go ahead." It was my mother's very proper voice sounding out from the living room, no more than three steps and a doorway away. "But, please keep an eye on them."

"I don't want to babysit the kittens, Mom. I want to decorate, too." I said as I rolled my eyes.

Big mistake.

"Attitude, Barbara." Oh, the whole name, not my nickname.

"Sorry," I said, staring down as the kittens scampered into the living room.

It was a playground for them. They hopped on top of garland and batted delicate glass balls over the carpet even as we grabbed them and called out.

"No!"

My father had the dubious task of unboxing the artificial tree and extracting the gazillion parts into some semblance of organization. Even now, I remember the muttering and cursing under his breath as he took each color-coded branch and laid them out to mark the layers that would eventually make the seven-and-a-half foot evergreen.

My brothers set out moving the chairs away from the wall and relocating them to a different part of the graciously-sized and extremely formal living room, dedicating an honored and important place for the tree so its splendor could be seen from any vantage point in the room. Everything was carefully choreographed by my mother.

After about two hours, the tree was ready to decorate. My dad was off duty now. My sisters took charge of the dining room, under the direction of my mother, of course. They set about placing the pine garlands on the hutch and fruited ones on top of the mirror above the buffet. The grandfather clock in the corner had its own festive wreath and bow. Meanwhile, "Joy to World" was coming from the huge stereo, a big long box, which sat on the front wall.

I was removing more of the tree ornaments as the kittens hopped into the boxes and fought for the most desirous ribbons and bows I pulled out. The kitties were mewing and hissing at one another.

Suddenly, there was a high-pitched shriek. My brother, Gus, accidentally stepped on the orange and white kitten, Tarzan. We had named him such because he was the runt of the litter and, for a while, we weren't sure he'd make it. We wanted to give him something to aspire to which was a name to give him courage and strength. He was much stronger now and played as much as the other kittens. At five weeks, no one could tell he had been the smallest.

Gus was always tender-hearted toward animals, so he quickly reached down to examine the little guy's foot. Tarzan squirmed and kicked, wanting to get back into the fun.

"You're okay, big boy," Gus said, setting him down into my lap as I sat on the floor.

Mom and my other brother, Christopher, set to putting the lights on the tree. Dad sat at his spot on the couch overseeing the entire operation.

Yiayia, my grandmother, who lived with us, was busy in the kitchen making coffee and plating cookies. She brought a piping hot cup of coffee into the living room for Daddy, along with the plate of *kourambiedes* (Greek festive butter cookies, covered with powdered sugar), setting them in front of him on the coffee table. She loved spoiling us, but she particularly enjoyed pampering her son-in-law.

Yiayia sat down on the other couch in front of me and Channie quickly snuggled up against her. Yiayia put her hand into her crochet bag and pulled out a ball of bright blue yarn, tossing it to the far side of the living room. Then, she threw a red ball of yarn, as well, before removing her needle and the blanket she was working on.

Soon, the eight kittens were unraveling the yarn balls, getting caught in the threads, and swatting one another. They bit and kicked each other, screeching and hissing above the background singing of "O Holy Night."

On the far side of the living room sat my father, his eyes closed now as he savored the rich, buttery cookie and sipped his coffee. After setting his cup down on the porcelain saucer, he looked up and shook his head.

"Not like that, Margaret. Those lights won't stand a chance if you don't anchor them down better. Twist them around the branches. It won't look good otherwise and you know those kittens are going to get into the tree and pull the lights off."

"I hadn't thought about that," Mom said.

At this point, my dad got up and took over. "Let me have this," he said and started from the top twining the light cords with precision around the tree, strand after strand until it was complete. "Ready to test?" he called out.

Christopher nodded and turned on the switch. Every light was evenly and securely placed, giving off a warm hue to the side of the room.

"Now, that's the way to do it," Dad said as he plopped a kiss onto Mom's ready lips.

A new record dropped onto the turntable of the stereo and we heard the Roger Wagner Chorale's "Sing We Now of Christmas." Dad threw another log onto the fire and poked it, sending the flames high up. He closed the mesh screen, turning his head to make sure the kittens were safely away.

One by one, the golden ornaments were strategically placed on the tree. The bells, the gold, and crystal tear drops, the golden fruit, and glittering angels. There were silver and gold balls looking like the onion domes of St. Basil's Cathedral in Moscow. There were pointy and elliptically-shaped ornaments hanging on golden thread glowing in the surrounding light. My mother stepped back admiring her creation as it evolved, one piece at a time.

It didn't take long for the kittens to appreciate the tree, as well. Branch by branch, they made their way into the tree, some of them sitting there like little lions. My sister, Michele, smiled at her favorite, Moonshine, the black, tan, and gold tortoiseshell, where she sat beneath the tree with her paws tucked snuggly beneath her.

"Look how she matches the tree. Isn't she cute?" I asked.

Everyone nodded in agreement, gazing lovingly at the baby cat under the tree. Everyone, except my father. He squinted at one branch and then another. There was a ping of a ball as it flew off the tree and hit the carpeted floor. First a gold glass ball and then the thud of the heavier crystal ones. Then, there was the clinking of the lead crystal teardrops.

"Get the cats off the tree, boys," Dad ordered.

My brothers hopped to action, laughing wildly as the cats responded with protesting meows and clinging claws, annoyed to be taken away from their rightful perches.

Channie jumped from the blue sofa where she'd been sitting. One by one, she carried her babies by the scruff of the neck back into the dining room. We replaced the dropped ornaments and soon the tree was decorated except for the final crowning touch. The room was quiet except for the music of "There Little Drummer Boy" in the background.

"Where's the topper?" my mother asked.

"Here, Mom," said Chrysie, the eldest. She pulled the special decoration out of the elongated box. It was a tall copy of a gilded Faberge tree topper that looked like an onion dome on a spire.

Dad took it and placed it firmly on the top.

We oohed and ahhhed at the sheer beauty of the luxurious tree.

My father was not so enthused, though. "Sheesh... How the heck are we going to keep those cats off the tree?"

"It'll be fine, Stanley. We'll just have to watch them."

"Who's going to guard them at night?" he wanted to know. "We'll have to put them in the laundry room."

My siblings and I cried out. "That's really mean, Dad. You can't do that. It's like punishing Channie."

"We'll figure it out. See? They're fine," my mother assured us.

My father shook his head and threw his arms up. "For now."

"Time to put the boxes away. Let's snap to it," Mother said to us.

We gathered the boxes and put them back into the storage closet. The coats were neatly returned to the closet, candles placed in the windows, wreath on the front door, with red bows on the outside lamps. Our home had been transformed into a winter wonderland.

The afternoon melted into evening with the kittens playing on or around the tree. Each time he heard the clinking ornaments, my father would cringe. Whoever was closest would go get the kittens off the tree.

At dinnertime, it was my job to be tree monitor, because my spot at the table happened to be near the doorway to the living room. After a while, the kittens were napping and had taken to the lower branches and the tree skirt beneath the tree.

The adults carried their evening coffee into the living room with us kids following along. There was more Christmas music put on the stereo and we played Monopoly as my parents and grandmother chatted. Channie sat near the hearth, drifting off into sleep.

"Oh, I almost forgot!" exclaimed my mother as she ran upstairs. She was back down in a flash, carrying a shopping bag.

"What's that?" asked my dad.

"Doves. Aren't they beautiful? I found a dozen of them at Hunter's. They look real. I thought they'd be gorgeous on the tree. See the clip on the feet? Help me put them on, will you, Stan?"

Soon, the birds were evenly placed on the tree with one right under the topper. We resumed our game of Monopoly and my mother refilled the coffee cups. Some time passed.

Then, we heard it.

At first, it was a faint meow. Then, there came the rustling of branches. There seemed to be a chorus of clickety-clacking cat noises. Little paws batted at the recently placed birds. One of the kittens had its "prey" clenched between its teeth and jumped down with it.

Mother screamed out, "No! Stop that."

"They don't understand you, Margaret," my father said with a smirk.

Feathers flew.

Branches bent.

The ornaments fell from the tree one-by-one as my mother's jaw dropped. My sisters and I giggled and my brothers rolled on the floor hooting with guffaws. Even my grandmother, who was usually reserved, squeaked out a laugh.

Dad threw his hand onto his forehead and stood up. "Get those things off the tree. Now!"

Too late.

At this point, the tree started to wobble. Tarzan and Coco had made it to the top and were fighting over the highest birdie. They hissed and growled, swatting at one another and moving with ease from branch to branch, each vying for the prize at the top. With this clatter, Channie woke up and meowed again and again until she gazed up at me pleadingly. By this time, everyone was standing. The striped kitten joined in the fracas and now there were three of them at the top.

The tree began to sway.

Gus called out, "Timber!" just as the tree went down.

"Shit!" my dad screamed.

The clatter of shattered ornaments filled the air as the tree whooshed by us to land in the center of the living room.

Channie jumped in, frantically seeking her babies. We found each one and placed them in their box. The last of them to be found was Coco. Even as my father jerked up the tree from the floor, Coco clung to the top. Her teeth were sunk into the neck of a birdie ornament.

"Get. The. cat. Down," my dad hissed through his clenched teeth.

"Come here, Tree Topper," Gus said as he unclipped the bird, still stuck in Coco's mouth. He took her back to her mama. Channie bit the fake bird and yanked it out of her mouth, spitting it onto the floor. She then snapped a scornful nip at Coco who retreated to a corner of the box. The other kittens found their way to their mama and began nursing.

The room was now silent.

My sisters and I cleaned up the broken ornaments while my father hammered nails into the tree base to secure it to the floor. He wrapped a string of fishing line around the top branch and attached it to a hook he'd placed in the ceiling. There would be no more disasters like this one again.

The tree would never be the same two days in a row that year. My mother gave up on having a picture-perfect tree. To me, it was unflawed, though.

I've gone on to have my own cats and you guessed it: Yes, we have a hook in our ceiling to secure the Christmas tree.

Every time I look up at it, I remember and laugh at the memory of those precious Tree Toppers.

Chapter

6

Barbie Dolls for Christmas

Cindy Clark

December 2017
Scottsdale, Arizona

I t was early on Christmas Eve and I smiled as I navigated my way through the busy Scottsdale traffic. I had just left Target where I'd bought the final Christmas presents—two "Holiday Collection" Barbie dolls.

Everything at home was ready for our traditional Christmas celebration. The dolls would join the other presents beneath the tree.

Our two sons, Lyle and Elton, now grown men, would be arriving from Los Angeles and Boston with their significant others that afternoon. Once everyone was there, we would start our traditional Christmas Eve celebration—first dinner and then gifts. I ticked off everything on my Christmas list.

The final thing was the Barbie dolls.

They were for Lyle and Elton.

Yes, for Lyle and Elton.

I honestly do not remember exactly how I came up with the idea to give my boys a Holiday Collection Barbie doll for Christmas. I think I read somewhere about a mother giving her sons a "girly" Christmas gift so she could get her girl "fix" because she'd never had one.

I must confess I'd always thought how fun it would be to have a girl and buy her girly gifts. But, I never did. My pride and joy were my two handsome, gifted, boys.

I also have a faint memory of telling them one Christmas how they would never be without a girlfriend at Christmas because *she* (the Barbie doll) would be waiting under the tree.

My boys have always known I was a bit nuts, so I do not think they were totally shocked to find Barbie dolls on Christmas morning. They always had grins on their faces and deep down inside, they were probably dying of laughter.

They have shared the Barbie story with many of their friends, so, obviously, they got a hoot out of it. Perhaps I created a unique Christmas tradition, and one day, they might do the same with their boys.

Some twenty-five years later, the tradition still continues in our family. I have a storage locker full of Barbie dolls. I probably have more than fifty Holiday Collection Barbie dolls in their unopened boxes. Yes, for some reason... our boys never took their dolls home.

I tease the boys that the dolls are their retirement investments. Some of them could fetch a hefty price if resold to a collector or on an online auction site.

So, maybe I'm not so crazy after all.

I read an article recently about a woman who gave stuffed bears to her family each Christmas until her house was overrun with the collectible teddies. She decided to take her collection and donate them to a children's hospital, which I thought was a lovely move.

Hmm...

I think I might just do that, too...

Christmas Fudge for Bismarck

Erika De Wet

Christmas Eve, 1994
Pretoria, South Africa

I n my mind, I couldn't get over the fact that Christmas time was so different between the southern and the northern hemisphere—one held inside, around the fireplace, with the snow falling softly, the other, outside, in the pool and around the barbeque. The common theme, though, would be to have your family with you wherever you might be.

In the background, the angelic voices of the Vienna Boys Choir could be heard and when the bells started ringing, announcing the old *Stille Nacht, Heilg'e Nacht*, a silence broke over the chit chatter of everyone present. This song, translated into so many languages and sung by so many people, symbolized Christmas to me.

An enormous Christmas tree stood proudly in the center of the sitting room. A whole world decorated its branches with Christmas decorations collected from everywhere we'd visited; each telling their own story. Subtle, tiny, twinkling lights contributed to the atmosphere.

Around the tree, ever so pretty, were Christmas presents waiting to make someone happy. Gifts, no matter how big or small, were chosen with love and care and placed under the tree. Some were more special than others because they were made by children for their parents.

The smell of cinnamon in the Glühwein, (German mulled wine perfect for cold winter weather), also contributed to the Christmas feeling. Most of all, it was being with family that made this Christmas so special. The previous two years, my husband, Daniel and I, celebrated Christmas on our own while he was studying abroad. Although we knew we were in our family's thoughts and they were in ours, it just wasn't the same.

Earlier, in the balmy afternoon, everyone was outside – the lapa (patio) and the swimming pool were the focal points. The sun danced on the brilliant blues and turquoises of the water. Shouts and laughter filled the air. Children squealed as they were tossed into the air by their dads. Who was going up the highest? Who could do the most summersaults? Who could hold their breath the longest?

After the fun in the water, it was time for dinner and what else could it be but a braai (barbeque). Steak, chops, boerewors (farmers sausage), krummelpap (porridge) with tomato and onion sauce, salads, roosterkoek (grilled bread), desserts, like koeksisters, malva pudding, and peppermint crisp tarts would follow after the presents, much later.

When nobody could eat another morsel and the kids couldn't contain their excitement anymore, it was time for the gifts. Even Bismarck, our Weimaraner, was seen going in and out the room as if to check and see if everything was ready.

But, we had to wait a bit longer, as a certain visitor was not yet there.

Just then, fortunately, the doorbell rang.

Bismarck got to the door first.

The kids were encouraged to go greet the special guest.

There stood Father Christmas. (No one realized Oupa had made himself scarce earlier.)

Wow... were we not the luckiest family? Father Christmas joined *us* tonight.

Slowly, everyone gathered around the tree. The little ones moved closer and the parents settled on the sofas. As in other years, Ouma read the story of the birth of Christ from the Bible. Then, she turned to Father Christmas and said, "You're on."

However, he was busy looking through his pockets. Oh, dear, did he forget his glasses? How would he be able to read the names? After a few tense moments, he found his spectacles.

"Ai, Oupa."

For the next couple of hours, you could hear the laughter and thank yous and see faces lit up like lightning in the sky. Small hands needed help to open the presents.

A few minutes were given to enjoy the pleasure of seeing someone opening his or her gift. It wasn't merely the children who received them. Every male in the family was surprised with a beautifully wrapped box containing homemade fudge given to them by my sister-in-law. It was the most delicious delicacy made of cream, butter, and sugar.

Father Christmas neared the end of the presents when suddenly, Marius, my brother-in-law, shouted, "Where's my fudge?"

No one confessed to taking it. Kids were ready to go and look for it, but in a silent moment, we heard it ...

...the distinct smacking of lips.

We turned as one and there, in the corner, stood Bismarck, licking his lips with a look of pure pleasure on his face. The box that had once held the beautiful homemade fudge sat in front of him... empty.

He was a smart one. A bone? A ball? No... that was not enough for him. He wanted fudge for Christmas.

And fudge he would get because he, too, was a male at the end of the day, wasn't he?

Chapter

Rudolph Cookies and a Shiny Disco Shirt

Lizel Sillman

Christmas 2013
Moultrie, Georgia

The first Christmas with my husband, Josh, was quite funny.

Josh wanted to make a good impression on his new stepson, Johan, who was still really big on Santa.

Josh's first lesson in Christmas etiquette happened when we were still engaged.

He offered to take four-year-old Johan to buy me a Christmas gift. In the small town where we lived, Walmart was the only store within a fifty-mile radius. So, Josh let Johan pick a gift and they wrapped it together when they got home.

Both of them were extremely impressed with themselves and their choice of gift. It was a real bonding experience for them.

However, on Christmas morning, we began to open our gifts.

Josh obviously had doubts with a look of, "Uh, I don't think you'll like it, but the kid picked it out."

Johan, on the other hand, had a giant smile on his face and was excitedly watching as I started to unwrap.

I ripped away at the paper and looked down. It was a sparkly disco ball staring back at me. I tore away the rest of the paper and saw it wasn't a disco ball, it was actually a shirt.

I wanted to give my fiancé the "Are you kidding me?" glare, seriously wondering if my choice of husband-to-be was a wise one. However, I smiled instead because Johan was so excited and screeched, "It is so *booooootiful,* Mommy. Put it on! Put it on!"

So, off to my room I went and returned wearing the sequenced shirt that would only be welcomed at a 1970s disco party. I laughed so hard tears were rolling down my cheeks. I rocked that disco ball shirt for a whole day, wearing it for two reasons: to spite my fiancé and to please my child.

Ever since then, Josh decided to choose the gifts as I made it very clear I would not like a matching pair of pants the following Christmas.

Josh's second lesson in Christmas etiquette came during the first holiday season after we got married.

Johan and I baked Rudolf-shaped cookies for Santa. After icing them, Johan put them out for Santa along with a glass of milk.

As I mentioned, Josh was trying to not disappoint his new stepson in any way. Added to this, he was totally new to the whole tradition of Santa and leaving cookies out for him. So, he winged it.

Johan went to bed with me in tow because he couldn't fall asleep from the excitement. That was when Josh went to town playing the role of Santa and chomping down cookies. These were not small cookies, either. They were monstrously huge and covered in an inch of icing... all four of them.

As I return to the living room, my beloved was sitting there about to get sick as he kept eating these gigantic cookies. He was determined to only leave a small bite of the final one. Santa had to show how much he loved the cookies Johan had left for him.

I smiled at Josh and said, "You know, you only needed to take one bite, right?"

Needless to say, three cookies in, Josh was green from eating the rich icing and washing it down with milk.

Now, several years later, and having been blessed with another little boy, my husband is much more familiar with our Christmas traditions, but we still laugh at those first Christmases together.

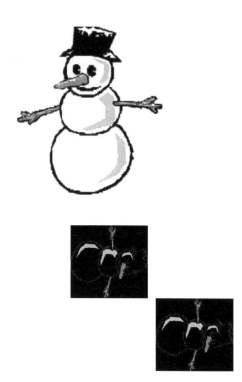

Chapter

9

The Sunflower Hat

Margaret Zeemer

December 1995
Florida

I was grocery shopping when I first saw it. Nestled high up on a rack stacked with Christmas ribbons and decorations at the end of the long aisles at Albertsons.

So out of place among the red and green display, the bright yellow and brown sunflower caught my eye and I stopped dead in my tracks to look at it more closely.

The sunflower was attached to a jolly-looking green gingham ribbon sprinkled with more sunflowers and the whole, silly spectacle was wrapped around the crown of a straw hat, the kind we city folk believe cowboys wear.

Crowded in amongst the shiny balls and silver bells, I reached to pick it up and knew I had to have it. I pushed my cart along the crowded aisle searching for a mirror so I could examine this new treasure on my head. I finally found one among the hair rollers and brushes. Self-consciously, I popped the hat onto my head, loving how well and comfortably it fitted me. Smiling again, I checked the price... only $7.99. What a deal. I dropped the hat into my cart and headed for the produce aisle.

Christmas in Florida was always a crazy time of mixed emotions and my current mood did nothing to lessen the stress of the seasonal demands. In a few days, I would be leaving for a trip to New York to visit good friends for the holiday weekend and looked forward to it with great excitement. I'd only been able to take three days off of work, so a small carry-on bag would be sufficient, I decided to wear a new denim outfit together with my freshly acquired hat for the trip. The temperatures in New York were already close to freezing and more bad weather was forecasted.

"Better take a coat," I thought.

But first, duty called.

I had to go to work on the day of my departure, so I had to plan my time appropriately. As usual, I started out early—four a.m. to be exact. After my o.j. and vitamins, I spent a short time going over last minute chores.

I share my home and life with a grand old Basset Hound I recently adopted. Rodney is an absolute sweetheart and loves to go on long walks and be told how wonderful he is. This morning, he seemed to sense something out of the ordinary for he was particularly lazy and aloof, using every ounce of his doggy guile to instill guilt in me for daring to leave him behind.

This, added to my usual routine of getting ready caused me so much delay I was horribly late for work.

Well, the whole day went downhill after that with one crisis after another.

I worked in the Intensive Care units of a large children's hospital in Florida and, for the most part, my years there have been happy and fulfilling. I have had the privilege of caring for so many wonderful babies and young children, many of whom were too sick to survive, but nevertheless, I felt blessed to be a part of the time they had here.

Such was this particular day, multiple and repeated emergencies, each one building upon the next. I was glad I had arranged to leave early, for tensions were high and so was my anxiety about possibly missing my flight. All this added to the negativity I was already allowing to grow inside of me. I felt as though a giant magnet had filled me and the more anger and frustration I felt, the more negative things kept happening. I was actually drawing bad things toward me.

I raced home under a grey and threatening sky. Of course, now it was going to storm and delay my flight. After such a terrible day, what else could go wrong?

The answer waited at home.

Recently I had rented a charming cabin in the mountains of North Carolina from a friend and had regretfully neglected to return her keys and linens to her. Her sweet voice echoed through my answering machine stating she had rented the cabin again and simply *must* have everything back before Saturday. This would add a full thirty minutes of travel time to the airport, but there was no avoiding it. It was my responsibility.

The drive to return her items to her office was a nightmare and it seemed as though every bad, rude, and ignorant driver had chosen that moment to be in my path. My anger grew as the seconds ticked by. The storm clouds loomed dark and heavy as I drove across Tampa Bay to the airport and matched my spirits.

Fortunately, I had no bags to check and so, after parking the car, I threw my hat on my head and raced to the gate, sure I would miss my flight, or worse yet, the ever-threatening weather would force me to miss my connection to Philadelphia and I would be stranded.

I stared up at the departure monitor in disbelief. Sure enough, my flight was delayed because of bad weather in the northeast.

I forced myself to sit quietly in the terminal and pulled out a book to read while I waited. I'm quite sure I re-read the same passage twenty times, at least. Adding to my unhappy state was the realization I had not eaten anything since early morning and had only the dubious airline food in my future. I was tired and irritable and my journey had just begun.

Finally, it was time to board and we were off. We arrived in Philadelphia safely and, miracle of miracles, I was in time to transfer to the flight to Long Island where my friends would be waiting for me (hopefully with a large scotch in hand.)

We had a short wait in the lounge and I found a seat against the wall next to a large plastic Christmas tree decorated with shiny balls and twinkling lights. I'd completely forgotten it was Christmas in two days. Right now, I was simply miserable and wanted nothing more than a cup of tea, a shoulder to cry on, a hot bath, and sleeeeeep.

The flight was called at last and I joined the rest of the weary travelers as we filed out of a door and were ushered by a rather bored looking airline official onto a waiting bus. It was dark by now and the freezing rain was coming down in buckets. We crowded into the drafty vehicle and were whisked off across the tarmac supposedly in search of our aircraft.

In the dim light of the bus, I became faintly aware of the other passengers, some of whom chatted away. Most, like me, seemed to be exhausted travelers anxious to get to their destination. Across the aisle, an elderly lady sat facing me. Something made me glance over at her as she sat clutching a battered leather handbag to her chest with a thin, worn raincoat the color of ashes draped across her lap.

As we drove past a fluorescent lamp post, the bus was suddenly filled with light and I saw her tired, wrinkled face and sensed an unbearable sadness there. Her eyes were filled with pain as tears ran down her pale cheeks.

The bus slowed to a stop. As the doors swung open, I bent to find my small bag. I glanced up at the woman again, but somehow she seemed different. The pain in her eyes was replaced with something new and there was almost a glow coming from her. She rose from her seat and came toward to me, a smile lighting up her wrinkled face as she squeezed my arm gently.

"I want to thank you," she said to me. "You will never know what seeing that sunflower has meant to me today. Thank you for wearing it."

My hat? I'd forgotten I even had it on.

So often, we forget how the smallest thing can affect the people around us, lives we never know we've even touched.

That rainy night on a bus in dismal Philadelphia, I remembered my sunflower. My self-indulgent gloom was lifted and I felt full of the joy of Christmas again.

I never saw that old lady again, although I was sure she boarded the same plane as me. Somehow, it didn't seem to matter.

I had been given a great and valuable lesson and I suddenly felt so much happiness that I laughed out loud.

My life was wonderful again and my $7.99 special was worth its weight in gold.

Chapter

10

Furry Escapades
Deb Rockwell

Christmas 1969
Columbus, Ohio

I t was Christmas and I was thirteen years old when I spent the night with my buddy, Junie.

Our mothers worked together at a place called Kings Answering Service. We met and became fast friends, spending all our days and most of our weekend nights at each other's houses. We would dream about the future, look through fan magazines, talk about boys, and argue over which Osmond brother we would marry... Donny or Jay.

This particular night, we were at Junie's house. It was dark outside and we were daydreaming in front of the Christmas tree in her living room.

Junie turned excitedly toward me and asked, "Do you want to see my mother's fur coats?"

"Of course," I practically screamed with excitement. For a girl of thirteen, fur coats meant stars and Hollywood. I couldn't believe Junie hadn't told me about them before.

She went to the closet and pulled out two brown coats with matching furry hats. They were beautiful. We proceeded to admire each other in the awe-inspiring garments. Then, we had the great idea to take a walk and enjoy the Christmas lights and let everyone else look at *us*. But it was dark and cold, so there would be no one out there. However, we would not let that deter us. We were looking good.

We bundled up against the cold winter air and started out on our stroll. It had snowed earlier that day and the Christmas lights sparkled on the snow. Junie's neighborhood was your usual 60s style set up with one-story houses, back-to-back with chain link fences blocking off each perfectly squared backyard.

The night was quiet and still as we walked around admiring the Christmas decorations, feeling like we were movie stars.

Most homes back then would put up one or two strands of lights with a lit Santa or Snowman on the porch if they were extra creative. It was a simpler time—sweet and understated.

As we turned the first corner, a dog's bark broke the silence. We thought nothing of it because most everyone had a friendly dog as a standard part of the family. So, we continued to walk. But soon we heard another dog barking. We glanced back and saw the first dog had jumped the fence and was heading right for us. We began to move a bit faster. By the time we rounded the next corner, a second dog had joined the first. We had the great idea to run.

The dogs did, too.

We laughed but then screamed, not sure if the friendly neighborhood dogs might not be so friendly.

"Help, help!"

"We're being attacked by dogs!"

We must have seemed like bears to the dogs, all bundled up in our fur coats and hats. Junie darted for a gate to the backyard of the nearest house. She knew they had a double-sided ladder we could climb over to get to the next yard.

We moved toward the ladder as fast as we could, yelling all the way. As we hit the ladder we were pushing each other out of the way to be the first over. Junie won and she literally flew over.

I was over on the other side of the fence when one of the dogs caught the edge of my huge fur monstrosity and started to hump it. I pulled away, screaming and laughing. I took one step and fell right on my face into the snow. I stretched my arm out for Junie, laughing uncontrollably, "Help me, save me!"

She yelled, "You are on your own... every man for himself."

I jumped up and soon caught up to her. A man peeked out his door to see what the yelling was about. We both began screaming together.

"We're being chased by dogs... help!"

We must have seemed crazy standing there in our wet furs, giggling. He sighed, shut the door, and turned off the light. We stared at each other for a minute and started laughing again.

We turned toward the fence and could barely see the dogs in the dark, barking and struggling to get over. So, we ran until we reached Junie's front door. We scrambled inside and fell on the floor in a heap. We told her Dad the whole ordeal, talking a hundred miles a minute.

He shook his head and said, "Take off those fake furs and hang them up to dry. I'll make you both something warm to drink."

We swapped glances and simultaneously said, "Fake furs?"

We ended up back in front of the Christmas tree drinking hot chocolate and giggling about our winter walk that had—literally—gone to the dogs.

11

Father Christmas Knows Where You Are

Drienie Hattingh

December 1980
Bryanston, Johannesburg, South Africa

W e were living in South Africa and were set to spend Christmas at our home in Bryanston, Johannesburg. However, early that morning, my husband, Johan, and I, changed our plans. We were used to having our family around at Christmas or being at the seaside in Durban, for the holiday vacation. This year, our brothers, sisters, and parents were on vacation and we were at home.

As the day wore on, we decided to accept my parent's invitation and join them at the Vaal River where they had rented a couple of bungalows. We told our two children, Eugene, six, and Brenda, four—both still strong believers in Father Christmas—about our new plans. They were extremely excited to visit Ouma and Oupa and spend Christmas with them.

Brenda, though, voiced her concerns.

"How will Father Christmas know where we are? I wrote him a letter and I put our house address on it. He will come to our house with our presents and we won't be here."

Eugene told his little sister, "Don't you worry, Brenda. Father Christmas knows everything. He will bring our presents wherever we are."

As we packed the car, Brenda was still hesitant.

"Are you sure, Eugene?" Concern was written all over her sweet face.

"Of course, I am, you'll see."

Johan took care to put Father Christmas's gifts into the trunk of our new beautiful metallic green Peugeot Sedan first, way back behind the luggage and other presents, so the children would not see them.

During our four-hour drive to Barage, the holiday resort on the banks of the Vaal River where my parents were, Brenda doubted whether or not Father Christmas would show up with their gifts.

My parents were extremely happy to see us pull up in front of their rented bungalows.

"You came!" Mother called out.

Pappie grabbed both Eugene and Brenda up in his arms as they exited the car and twirled around with them.

The excitement came to a halt when Johan wanted to unload our suitcases and... the presents. The trunk would not open. He kept turning the key every which way, but no luck. Unbeknownst to us, this particular model car was on the recall list because of the faulty trunk locks.

Johan let out a big grunt and needlessly said, "The presents are in the trunk."

Eugene and Brenda stood next to the car with Eugene playing with his yo-yo, letting it go up and down, up and down.

He turned to his sister and said, "We don't have to worry, Brenda. Father Christmas is bringing *our* presents."

Johan threw his hands up in the air in exasperation. It didn't help his anxiety when Pappie, bless his heart, walked up with a screwdriver. Oh dear. He was going to do his best to get the lock open, come what may.

Johan's face turned a deeper red when he saw my father's intentions, but, of course, he could not say anything to Pappie. That would be disrespectful.

As my determined father pushed the screwdriver into the lock, the tool accidentally slid, and it made a deep, long scratch on Johan's brand-new car.

My poor mother winced and reached out to draw my kids nearer. In a cheerful voice, she suggested, "Come on, Eugene and Brenda. You must be hungry. Let's go make some something to eat."

I followed everyone into the bungalow.

We had hardly started making sandwiches when Johan and Pappie walked into the bungalow with their arms loaded with luggage and Christmas presents.

"The trunk popped open all of a sudden," Pappie said with a laugh.

Johan seemed better, but I knew the scratch on his new car still hurt.

Nevertheless, the following night, as the kids dove into the sea of presents awaiting them, we had to listen to Eugene's gloating, as he told his sister time and again, "See, Brenda. I told you Father Christmas always knows where we are!"

He sure did.

Chapter

12

The Used Christmas Presents

Celeste Canning

November 1960
Syracuse, Utah

I t was a beautiful fall afternoon in early November. The air was crisp and clean, promising winter weather around the corner. It was not yet dark, but the evening was on its way.

Since Mom and Dad had gone to town and would be away for a while, I figured I had enough time to check the trunk of Dad's patrol car. My dad was the sheriff. I often found interesting things there. Well, mostly various guns, which were of the utmost interest to me.

My brother mostly went with me on these exploratory expeditions, but he wasn't around tonight. I chuckled, thinking it would be his tough luck if I found something interesting. He'd just have to check it out later if he could. These treasures might be gone the next day.

I pulled Dad's keys from where they were stored, while not in use, and made my way to his car. I popped the trunk, hoping to find a hunting rifle or maybe a pistol. Instead, I found a .22 rifle and a pellet gun. These didn't look like the tools of my father's trade or even hunting rifles.

I carefully withdrew the .22 rifle from the trunk and checked it out. It was a Browning, the sweetest .22 I'd ever seen. The pellet gun, still in the trunk, begged me to check it out, too. I inspected it as I leaned against the trunk. Then stood back, and admired them both.

I really wanted to shoot each of them. I dug around in the trunk. Sure enough, there was ammunition, too. One box for each gun.

The gears inside my head began to turn and I stood tall.

Can it be?

I had asked for a .22 for Christmas, but didn't really expect to actually get it. Christmas was still six weeks away, so this couldn't be my present. Also, even though I was a good marksman and always practiced safety with a gun, I was still only eleven years old.

My parents wouldn't really get me the gun, would they? No, they won't.

What were the guns doing in Dad's patrol car? Perhaps they were stolen guns he needed to return to the owners. What would be the harm in using it while it is here?

The more I stared at them, the more I thought. *Well, I am a really good shot. I am very safe with guns.*

Dad taught me and my brother how to shoot and how to do it right and safely.

It had been years since I'd shot the flies in the barn—and a few holes in the roof—but look at all the flies I got. On top of that, I've been really good this year. I broke the horses I was assigned this summer. I even did irrigating; only got caught sleeping by the ditch once.

I've worked really hard.

I deserve to have a bit of fun with the rifle, don't I?

The longer I thought, the more reasonable it seemed Mom and Dad (well, mostly Dad) would understand how I deserved to spend some time target practicing with this rifle. If he should catch me—if not... no harm done.

Yes, I'd worked hard for it and I deserved some fun. And if it was stolen property, where would be the harm if I put a few bullets through it?

No harm at all. None.

Heck, if it was so, and just sitting in the trunk, it was practically begging to be used.

Anyway... who would know? I could have the gun safely back in the box and tucked into the trunk before Dad got back from town. If I only shot one magazine, Dad might not even notice the missing bullets.

Having thought it through carefully, I nabbed the .22 and quickly loaded it. I placed a tin can on the fence post, backed up a few feet, squinted down the gun's site, and prepared to fire.

Kablam!

I didn't hit the can.

I fired again.

Kablam!

I didn't hit the can.

I fired again.

Kerchoow!

This time, I hit the edge of the can.

I fired again. And again. And again.

I had to reload the gun, but soon, I could hit the can almost every time. I moved back farther still hitting my target. I wanted to hit it every time, dead center, since my dad was a shooting instructor in the Army. He had high expectations of me whenever he let me shoot. I wanted to make him proud of me.

My little brother showed up, called by the siren song of the rifle. I showed him the other gun and its box of pellets. Of course, being the older brother and the one who'd found the guns, I had to try the pellet gun first.

I loaded the gun and fired a few pellets, hitting the target every time. The pellet gun was fun enough, but it couldn't compare to the .22. I reloaded both and handed the pellet gun to my brother to try. We continued to fire away.

The next thing I knew, it was getting dark and the box of bullets was empty.

Oh, no!

My plan had been to only fire a few rounds. I glanced over and saw the box of pellets was empty. My heart jumped to my throat and stuck in a big lump of anxiousness. I was going to be in so much hot water when Dad found out.

But wait, it was Friday which meant no school tomorrow.

I could ride my bike down to the local store and get more bullets and pellets. If I was really careful—and lucky—I could replace the boxes before Dad discovered they were empty. After all, Saturday was one of his days off, so it wasn't likely he'd check the trunk.

Right?

It would take most of the money I had, but it'd be well spent if I could pull it off.

I called my brother over and hurried and wiped the guns off, putting them oh, so carefully, back into their boxes. I stashed the empty ammo and pellet boxes back in the trunk, too. If Dad picked them up, he'd know something was up. I had to hope he just wouldn't even look in the trunk until I could make good on this.

I hardly slept that night. I would drift off only to be sure I'd heard the trunk pop open. I'd jump out of bed, run to the window, and… nothing. Dad wasn't in the yard, nor was the trunk open.

I hadn't been caught.

Not yet.

I drifted back to sleep, but then I thought I heard the front door open.

My heart was racing like a locomotive, but it was simply another false alarm.

Or, maybe, my conscience was getting the best of me?

The next morning, I was a nervous wreck.

Worried Dad might discover what I'd done before I could get back from the store; I hurried through breakfast and then got right to my chores. Mom wondered what was wrong with me, but I had other things to worry about... like getting bullets and pellets back in the boxes before I was busted.

When I was done, I got on my bike and rode to the general store, a few miles away. I knew Joe, the store owner, would sell me the ammo I so desperately needed. He *had* to.

Trying to be cool, I went into the store.

"Morning, Matt," said Joe. "What can I help you with today?"

"Oh," I said, "I need a box of .22 shells and a box of pellets. Got any?"

Joe thought for a minute, and then replied "Long rifle? I believe I do. Let me go check."

He went into the back of the store where I could hear him talking to someone. I fidgeted in place, worried he wasn't going to sell me the bullets. I didn't hear anyone else's voice. Weird, I thought, I didn't hear the phone ring. However, thoughts of Joe's phone call went right out of my head when I saw he was carrying the shells and pellets I'd requested.

Yes! Phase one of my plan complete.

I paid for my booty, loaded it into my pockets, and headed for home.

Dad wasn't around when I arrived, so I got the keys, opened the trunk, removed the old boxes and carefully replaced them with the new ones. I shut the trunk quietly and looked around. I saw no one.

Phew!

I'd gotten away with it.

I swear, I'll never do that again.

That weekend, I opened the trunk every chance I got to look at the .22 and to make sure Dad hadn't taken them out. Every time, they were still there. This routine continued into the new school week.

All I could think about was that sweet .22.

What else can I shoot at?

I couldn't shoot birds or rabbits because I'd have to explain where they came from since we always ate what we shot (except varmints, of course). I could shoot more cans, but that was getting to be a bit boring since I hit it nearly every time. Finally, I decided, I could set up more than one can and rapid fire at them, switching things up.

Wait a minute. I'd sworn I wouldn't get the gun out again.

Back to paying attention to school, I went.

That only lasted a few minutes. Then, my mind drifted off to the .22 again. Hmmm... since I'd managed to pull it off once, maybe I could do it again. But, this time, I'd be smarter. I'd buy the bullets in advance. I'd wait until Mom and Dad left again, slip out, shoot a few rounds, and replace the spent bullets before they got home.

Dad would tan my hide if he caught me.

Back to school for a few minutes. But, I replayed the same conversation, justification, and plotting over and over again.

Before I knew it, the plot was hatched.

Friday morning, I made sure to ride my bike to school. I took the last of my money with me. In school, all I could think about was getting those bullets and shooting that sweet, sweet gun.

As soon as school was dismissed, I jumped on my bike and pedaled for all I was worth back to Jim's. This time, Jim didn't hesitate. He pulled the shells from under the counter.

"This what you're looking for?" he asked.

"Yes, thank you," I said, trying not to quiver from the excitement.

After paying Jim, I left the store and headed for home, hoping as hard as I could Mom and Dad would be gone again.

I was crushed to see Mom and Dad were home, Not that I didn't love them, but couldn't they, just this once, do what I needed? When I got in, Mom was talking.

"Bob, you know your sister is under the weather. I made some chicken soup, so how about we take it over to her? We can also check out the mare you were telling me about."

My dad looked at her, and then glanced at me. He winked.

"Sure," he said. "It's been a while since we've seen Bill, too. We can stop in to see him. It's right on the way to see the mare. We'll take the truck in case I can talk Bill out of those fence posts he's been holding on to."

Perfect, I thought to myself. It's at least a half-hour drive to Aunt Julie's, then another fifteen minutes to Bill's. They'd take at least another fifteen minutes to check out the mare, so, in total, I figured they'd be gone for two hours, maybe more. That was plenty of time for me to shoot, even after I got my chores done.

"You behave and be careful while we're gone," Dad said. "You make sure you take care of your brother and include him in whatever you do."

I stared at Dad. That wasn't like him. Normally, he'd remind me of the chores I had to do. Since when did I babysit my brother? Heck, since when did my brother need a babysitter? I wondered about it, but not for long. I hardly believed it. Dad hadn't given me any chores; all I had to do was take my brother with me, whatever I did. That would be easy. He'd have just as much fun the pellet gun as I'd have with the rifle.

I couldn't wait for my parents to get in the truck and drive away.

As soon as they were gone, I hollered for my brother.

When he came running, I showed him the .22 shells and pellets I'd gotten. His eyes got big and he raced me to the car. I hoped the guns were still there and Dad hadn't taken them out. Eyes aglow and fingers trembling, I put the key in the lock and turned it. *Yes!* The guns were still there. In no time we had them out of the trunk, loaded, and were firing away.

For the next several weeks, I daydreamed about the guns. I could only afford one box each of .22 shells and pellets. It stripped my savings, but it was worth it.

I shot at cans, fence posts, rocks, and sticks. I shot up close, far away, high, and low. I became a good marksman, hitting whatever I aimed for. I shot after school and on weekends, whenever Mom and Dad weren't home. I had to be careful to leave a full box of bullets in the trunk, but what a small price to pay.

Needless to say, I saw a lot of Jim. It became a ritual, my stopping in every Friday night to get shells. We'd talk for a few minutes, he'd pull the ammo out from under the counter, and I'd settle up. We'd say our goodbyes and I'd take off for home on my bike.

I didn't always get to shoot on Fridays, but I did get to shoot every weekend. A couple of times, I wondered how long this would last. I didn't know how long Dad would get to keep the guns, when he'd have to turn them in, or if he'd have to give them back to the owner. But, in those glorious days between Thanksgiving and Christmas, I didn't care.

On the last Saturday before Christmas, I was loaded with ammo waiting to see if Mom and Dad would leave again. I felt I was getting pretty darned good with the .22, and couldn't wait to get my hands on it. This weekend, I was going to try to shoot from horseback, my biggest challenge yet.

However, instead of leaving, Dad gave me a long list of chores to do. I worked mucking stalls, hauling hay, and feeding horses.

At first, I moved quickly so I could get my chores out of the way, leaving more time to shoot once Mom and Dad left. They had to go out, didn't they? I mean, it was the weekend before Christmas. Surely they had some shopping to do.

As the day wore on, despair set it. It was getting late and if my parents didn't leave soon, it would be too dark to see.

When my brother and I had all but given up hope, Dad called to Mom, "Sue, let's go to town, get a piece of pie and go visiting." Finally! Mom and Dad left, and my brother and I hurried to the barn to saddle the horses.

The experience was glorious. I shot from horseback. It was hard, but I hit my target a few times. I whooped and hollered every time I dinged the can, the rock, or the stick.

At last, we'd fired all our ammo. We cleaned up the horses and turned them into their stalls. We wiped down the guns and placed them back in the slightly worn boxes. We headed into the house and into bed.

Finally, Christmas morning came.

My brother, sister, and I opened our presents. I was a bit disappointed. My brother and I got socks, a shirt, and shoes, but nothing else. My sister got a lot more. Of course, as she never tired of telling me, she was older. She seemed to think that meant she deserved more.

As if.

I thought about whining, but before I could open my mouth, I thought better. If that was what we had, or what we could afford, whining wouldn't change anything. However, I tossed my sister a dirty look.

About that time, Dad came back into the living room. In his arms, he carried two boxes.

Long boxes. Skinny boxes. Gun boxes.

My heart dropped to the floor. I was busted, I just knew it. Dad had found out what I'd done, and that was why I didn't get much for Christmas.

But wait, Dad was smiling, a big grin, the kind that lit up the room.

"Boys," he said. "Gather round. I've got something here I think might interest you."

When I ran to him, he handed me a box. The .22 box. With the .22 in it.

"For me?" I asked.

He laughed and said simply, "For you, son. You've been a big help this year. I think it's time you moved up from the BB gun."

My mouth dropped open because it had never occurred to me the gun could be *my* Christmas present. I thought it was stolen guns. Dad had brought it home so early and left it in the trunk for so long.

Why would he do that?

I wondered. But I didn't wonder for long.

In no time, I was dressed and out the door with Dad and my brother following. We shot for a long time that day. Dad commented about what good marksmen we were, but I brushed it off. "I'm a natural," I said.

After we were done, Dad made me clean the .22 before putting it away for the night.

Many, many years later, when I was a full-grown man, with children of my own, Dad turned to me one day and asked, "So, how many bullets did you put through that old .22 before Christmas, anyway?"

As I've aged, I've thought about and shot that sweet .22 often. Always with a smile while I reminisced about my Dad and my brother, both of whom I stayed close with until they each died.

That experience formed the adult I would become in so many ways.

I still get into Christmas presents early, although now they were for my children and grandchildren. If the present required skill, I opened it up and tried it out long before Christmas.

My kids and grandkids always wondered why I was so good at the new video games right out of the box.

What could I say?

Wishing You a Wonderful Christmas

Chapter

13

Pumba the Potbellied Piggy

Juli Robertson

December 2002
Pretoria, South Africa

I 'd always wanted a potbellied pig.

After years of begging my husband, Lance, he relented and, in 2002, and we set about finding one. We eventually found a miniature Vietnamese Potbellied Pig and brought him home to our guest house in Pretoria, South Africa, where we lived at the time.

What a cutie he was.

You guessed it, we named him Pumba, being an African cousin.

Pumba settled in and saw me as his mama. He also took a liking to our Great Dane, Madam, who was also black in color like him.

Pumba would run through the guest house to everyone's delight. His little feet would wheel spin on the marble tiles like a cartoon character.

My sons immediately loved him, of course.

Pumba would explore every inch of the guest house and our 2.2-hectare property. But, he had a little problem which would turn out to be a big problem—he ate everything in sight and even challenged the dogs for their food. Pumba grew fatter and fatter and no longer looked like his miniature Vietnamese cousin. His tummy drooped lower and lower.

Pumba got into more and more mischief. He would dig up everything with his snout, which didn't endear him to Lance and the gardeners. Lance would at Pumba and he would react by wanting to bite Lance. I, it seemed, was the only one who could discipline fatty, Pumba. After I'd reprimand him, he would walk away sniffling like a punished child.

Eventually, Pumba got so big and fat we no longer allowed him inside the guest house. He would knock over small tables and even little children as he ran from room to room. He still acted as if he was a small piggy, and did not seem to know he was really big now.

One of the incidents with our dear Pumba was some years later on Christmas Eve when we traditionally handed out our gifts. We always put up our tree the second week of December. As each family member bought and wrapped their gifts, they placed it under the tree.

On this specific Christmas Eve, someone had left an outside door open and Pumba strolled into the house. He must have been thrilled to see the Christmas tree with its sparkling lights and the gifts around it.

Later that afternoon, Lance walked past the tree and noticed some of the boxes looked like they had been kicked around. Upon closer inspection, we noticed almost every gift bag and/or box had been torn, ripped, and broken. Some of the gifts were lying outside the bags. I had bought my son's special t-shirts with funny logos. These were now lying around with slime, mud, and goo all over them.

The gifts had clearly been dragged around and shaken. Delightful smelling perfume, hand creams and powder, obviously meant for me, and cologne for Lance was spilled out over the floor and over other presents in various states of disrepair. The glass and carton containers were broken and chewed.

Lance and I observed the spectacle in utter amazement and shock. Then we looked at each other and mouthed the same single word.

"Pumba!"

I went hunting for the pig and found him sitting under a shady tree, seeming pleased with himself, smelling wonderful. I almost did not recognize him because he was no longer black; he was white, covered in powder and had blobs of hand-cream all over.

I shouted, "Pumba, what have you done?"

He whimpered and sniffled like a child. He tried running away and hiding, to get away from me, but he could no longer run fast because his belly was too large and too low on the ground. He turned away in shame and did a type of a lengthways split with his front paws forward and back paws backward. He tried to slide away from me on his belly.

I burst out laughing.

Regardless of the mess he'd left behind and ruining our Christmas Eve celebration, this was simply the most hilarious sight I'd ever seen.

That night, we all had to accept our Christmas gifts in the ruined state they were. We did not have time to buy anything else or even wash our boys' t-shirts, so they received them covered with slime, muck, and dirt. However, we could not stop laughing whenever we thought of our poor "little" Pumba, wallowed in shame.

We had a great time at dinner that night, recalling all the mischief our beloved potbellied piggy, gotten himself into.

Chapter

14

Christmas Was a Bummer

Alex Montanez

December 1952
Ogden, Utah

As I reflect on my childhood, I have many fond memories and some not-so-fond memories.

One Christmas, when I was a preschooler, I was super excited because the largest present under the tree had my name on it. We were very poor at the time, but I didn't really get what it meant. I just knew there weren't many presents under our tree. So, this one definitely stood out.

Oh, I remembered it so vividly. We had one of those aluminum trees and an electric color wheel was placed on the floor to give the tree a tinted effect. The wheel spun around slowly, changing the hues of the tree effortlessly. I sat there, mesmerized, watching the different shades wash over the bulky present sitting right in front of the tree.

I begged my mom to let me open the present on Christmas Eve, but she stood her ground and tucked me in. As I lay in bed thinking about the possibilities were contained within the snowman-wrapping paper, I couldn't sleep. I tossed and turned and it was the longest night of my life.

When morning came, I peered out my window and saw a fresh blanket of snow. On that snowy morning, I tried to wake everyone, but they reacted by shrugging me off and continuing to sleep.

Finally, the family slowly came into the living room and my mom lit the gas furnace. It didn't take long for it to heat the whole house... I mean, it got hot.

When it was time to open presents, my mom could tell I was jumping out of my skin to open mine first.

She smiled at me and asked, "Well, what are you waiting for?"

I knocked over the color wheel to get to my gift. I ripped off the wrapping paper in a matter of seconds to reveal the most awesome fire truck I'd ever seen. This fire truck was huge and made entirely out of plastic. I started pushing it around on the floor, but that wasn't good enough.

I need to take this outside and try it in the cold wilderness.

Do you remember how the kid brother in *A Christmas Story* got wrapped up from head to toe in his cold-weather gear? That was no exaggeration. I didn't have snow boots, so my mom had to improvise with two empty Wonder

Bread bags to keep my feet dry. After putting on three shirts, two pairs of pants, and three pairs of socks—one pair on my hands as mittens, I was almost ready to go. The final touch was my shoes, coat, and a hat.

I grabbed my new fire truck and ran outside as fast as my legs would carry me. I jumped off the porch and into the crunchy new snow. I couldn't have been happier. Now, there was work to be done, people to be rescued, and cats to be saved from high trees. Yes, I was on a mission.

After playing with my shiny red truck I thought, *Mr. Truck, you look awfully cold. I should probably take you inside and get you warmed up.*

Brushing as much snow off my pants as I could, I rushed into the house to warm up my new red fire truck. I figured the best and fastest way to thaw my frozen truck was to get it as close to something really warm as I possibly could. So, I set it on top of the furnace in the living room.

I ran to my room to start the grueling process of peeling off my winter suit. Regardless of my mom's efforts, I was wet all the way through from playing in the snow, right down to my tighty-whities. So, I removed everything. When I got done, I noticed a funny smell coming from the living room.

I peeked around the corner to see my fire truck had almost completely melted on the furnace. The only thing remaining was the steel axels holding the tires together and a red pile of goo.

The only words I uttered were, "Uh, oh."

My mom came bounding into the living room, obviously smelling the burned plastic, and screamed, "What did you do?"

I was so startled, I backed right into the red, hot furnace and burned my tushy something fierce. I let out a blood-curdling scream and fell into my mom's arms crying... not so much from the burn, but from the loss of my beautiful, red, fire truck.

I learned two valuable lessons that day.

Number one: *You don't have to warm up inanimate objects.*

Number two: *Old furnaces are butt magnets.*

Chapter

15

Where's the Ham?

Penny Ogle

December 1985
Butte, Montana

From the time I was a child, the Christmas season was a cornucopia of special traditions. When I married, not only did the old traditions continue, but we added some of our own.

We anticipated opening advent calendar windows, searched for fun places for a picture on Santa's lap, went on family shopping excursions to select special presents for each other, wore pajamas on Christmas Eve, and Dad making "pull-apart" rolls for breakfast and ham with all of the "fixings" for dinner.

Christmas 1985 was difficult for our family. We'd left friends and family and moved to Butte, Montana. Our girls were away at college, so coming home for Christmas wasn't really "home" at all.

To create a new tradition, we bundled up in jackets, scarves, and mittens trudged into the snow-covered mountains to cut down a tree. Since we lived in what was once Evil Knievel's home, we decided to be a bit daredevil to break from tradition and decorate our beautiful fir tree with blue ornaments, clear glass balls, and mauve bows.

However, the sad faces of our children prompted me to get a second tree and load it with familiar and traditional ornaments. Santa pictures were a thing of the past, but we had our Christmas Eve PJs and our traditional Christmas Eve gift shopping.

In the 1980s, Butte had one small shopping center; but we headed out determined to find each other fun things.

The shopping excursion was a success, so we gathered back in the kitchen, laughing and comparing our gift buying successes. We had been able to create a tradition where only the unfamiliar had existed.

As I looked around, at the bags and packages, I wondered where the rest of the plunder had been stored. I found the sweet potatoes, rolls, and apples for applesauce... but where was the ham?

"Did you girls see the ham?"

"No," they answered in unison.

"You didn't put it up or anything?

They repeated their answer.

Further queries rendered similar responses. The boys hadn't seen the ham and my husband didn't even remember picking it up or bringing it in from the car. I'd specifically asked him to grab it for me, but he denied ever hearing the request. Thinking he must be teasing, I retraced my steps.

No ham.

Anywhere.

What was going on?

Sweet potatoes and rolls might pass for Christmas dinner any other time, but this year the news anchor for the local TV station was our guest.

What am I going to do?

After a morning of munching on pull-apart rolls and exclaiming over our gifts, I got serious about trying to create a traditional ham dinner without the star attraction. I couldn't pull a ham from thin air. Christmas was hard enough...but no Ham Dinner? Unthinkable.

No stores were open for miles around and most restaurants were closed for the holiday. Time was slipping by. What was I going to serve with the rolls and pumpkin pie?

I looked over my larder and discovered I had mushrooms, onions, celery, sausage, and even fresh oregano, everything for spaghetti. Spaghetti for Christmas Dinner, though? I didn't have a choice. Spaghetti would have to do. Even this dish was difficult because I barely had enough pasta. I would just have to serve it myself, making sure there would be enough for everyone.

So, I chopped and worked and soon had the sauce bubbling.

I cooked the noodles and. carefully poured them into the colander. I couldn't afford to let a single strand slip down the drain. Then, I squirted dish soap into the pan in preparation to soak the pan. I rinsed the spaghetti and poured it back into the pan to keep it warm. I was now ready to serve our Christmas dinner of spaghetti.

Everyone gathered around the table and I portioned out the spaghetti, not wasting a noodle. I was very proud of my sauce and decided this might be our new tradition, but the look on everyone's face was enough to cause concern. I took one bite and jumped up in panic.

"Soap!"

I had forgotten to rinse the pan out. Although I had plenty of sauce, I had no more spaghetti. Without so much as a blink, I picked up our guest's plate, dumped the contents into the strainer, washed the pasta clean, returned the well-rinsed spaghetti to her plate, added new sauce, and reserved it. I repeated this for everyone and everything seemed fine. Everyone dug in and I sat down in exasperation.

I reached for my wine and shook my head. "You can all now utter one bad word since you've already had your mouth washed out with soap."

Chapter 16

The Worst Christmas Presents Ever

Ilze Botha

December 1990
Skurwepoort, Cradock, South Africa

I was very much a city girl, so I was excited to spend my first Christmas as a married couple on my in-law's farm, Skurwepoort, in Cradock in the Eastern Cape of South Africa. Eastern Cape was also known as "The Karroo." The farm belonged to my brother-in-law, Penny Hattingh, and his wife, Lulu. They lived with their children, JC, Lanoy, and Penny's mother, Aunt Lenie.

If I'd known what was lying ahead, I would not have been so eager about the trip. I was about to learn more about my new in-laws, as well as how a perfect plan can go wrong on a Karroo farm.

Christmas on a farm in South Africa could be a joyous, fun, and exciting family gathering for grown-ups and children alike. First, the house was cleaned from top to bottom and then the fun started. Everyone received a brand-new outfit and the very best food was prepared, usually from scratch.

To impress my new in-laws, I offered to make a Christmas trifle, which is a cold dessert of sponge cake and fruit covered with layers of custard, jelly, and cream. Armed with meticulous "how to" notes from my mother, I felt confident in attempting this dessert.

The preparations for our festive meal on the farm were done the day before Christmas. Fixing a traditional holiday on a Karoo farm was an experience in and of itself. Everyone had a job to do. The men did their usual farm work. Christmas or not, animals still had to be fed, cows milked, fences mended, etc. The women prepared the food and set tables, and farm workers frantically ran around to finish cleaning in and around the house in preparation for the special day.

At noon, with everything completed, the farm workers and their families gathered in the garden under the trees. Everyone, young and old, then received a gift, sweets (candy), and a new outfit. Each family also received a food parcel that included a whole lamb. The workers and their families then entertain the farmer and his family and guests by singing traditional Christmas songs. On this day the workers' children got another special treat—a ride on the tractor to their homes. Finally, the workers got the rest of the day off to spend with their families.

After the heartwarming event outside, I returned to the kitchen to make my trifle. It turned out to be a masterpiece and I was feeling quite proud of my effort as everything was going according to plan. The custard, in particular, came out silky and smooth.

Not too bad.

Today, I would show the farm aunties that this city girl was okay.

To cool the custard down a bit quicker, I decided to put it on the window sill of an open window where a light breeze made its way through. I continued preparing the other ingredients.

In the rush to get the chores done, the workers were later than usual feeding the calves and lambs. One of the impatient calves, however, set out investigating what had happened to breakfast, passing the kitchen window where my bowl of custard was cooling down. He obviously smelled something heavenly and milky, so he stuck his head through the window and cleaned out the bowl.

The kitchen crew, startled by the sounds, stood in disgust as they watched the custard bowl make its emptiness dance across the kitchen floor. I was devastated. My marvelous custard found its way into the empty stomach of a cocky calf.

Fortunately, my sister-in-law, Lulu, took pity on me and together we made more custard so the trifle was saved.

At sundown, the men excused themselves and went to check on the sheep in the fields.

Upon their return, we had the long-awaited Christmas dinner.

When we could not eat even one more thing, the women and girls cleared the tables and then we all gathered around the piano to sing Christmas carols.

There was excitement in the air because it was time to unveil the gifts. Being the head of the house, Penny kept his gift until the very last. Proud and with fanfare, he presented his offering to his wife.

Wow, this is so romantic!

I hoped my new husband would be as romantic as his sister's husband.

With radiant appreciation in her eyes, Lulu accepted her present, heartily thanking Penny. She sat down and carefully opened the wrapped gift which seemed as if it might contain something like the most beautiful piece of jewelry.

I would never forget the look of disbelief on Lulu's face when the wrapping eventually came off. At first, I thought her reaction was because of a stunning present, but no. There on her lap, within the folds of the beautiful Christmas paper were... *a bar of soap and a washcloth.*

Flat lipped and silent, Lulu was not impressed.

Then, JC, not wanting to be outdone by his dad, pulled out his surprise gift to his sister, Lanoy.

A bottle of ketchup.

What?

At her obvious disgust, JC said, "But, you *love* ketchup."

I wasn't so sure that was still the case.

My husband told me later that Penny simply wasn't the romantic kind. He probably saw that his wife's washcloth needed replacing and thought it would be a nice touch to add a sweet-smelling bar of soap.

And, JC was always giving his sister gag gifts, so that explained that.

My first Christmas as a married woman went down in family history as the one with the worst gifts ever.

However, to end on a happy note…. On our first Christmas together, my new husband, Johan, gave me a beautiful gold chain.

As it happened, I *did* marry a romantic.

17

Christmas Veggies and a Three-legged Table
Mikki Ashton

December 1967
Spokane, Washington

A Christmas tradition in our family was going to my aunt and uncle's house in Spokane, Washington, where we were treated to the customary meal of turkey, stuffing, mashed potatoes, vegetables, rolls, and other holiday dishes. Including my sisters and cousins, there were seven children in attendance.

As we dished up our plates to the level of overflowing, our parents would dutifully watch over us to ensure we included helpings of vegetables along with the good (a.k.a. fattening) things. I thought we should get a no veggies pass for the special meal. However, I was too young to force a vote on it. So, I obediently put the offensive vegetables on my plate with the smallest helping possible that would hopefully pass my mother's close inspection.

Once we kids finished plating, we were instructed to take our heaping servings and our noisy selves downstairs to the family room to leave the adults in peace.

The family room was more of a repository of old furniture, bad carpeting, and seclusion from the adults' peering eyes. I didn't see it as banishment to a small, dim room, rather it was a sanctuary. Perhaps, I could even dump my veggies somewhere inconspicuous without an adult knowing... or finding out.

It was *perfect* for a seven-year-old like me.

Once downstairs, dibs were quickly made on the seating arrangements. Again, I didn't have much of a voice or vote in the matter. Since I was one of the youngest (and smallest) of the bunch, I was ordered to the corner of an old couch.

I was okay with that, but there wasn't a way to access the spot without first stepping on a side table. So, with a full plate in hand, I climbed onto the tabletop determined to get to my assigned seat and start my feast.

Unbeknownst to me (although I was sure my cousins knew), the table I was traversing across only had three legs—not very sturdy ones at that. As soon as I stepped on the handicapped table, I went down TKOd prizefighter and my plate full of food went up in the air and did a diver's double-tucked pike.

Turkey and stuffing landed *splat* on the carpet, potatoes *smacked* up on the walls, as well as all over my arms, and the thick gravy *plopped,* saturating my hair. The freshly-baked roll shot torpedo-like behind a lamp and the various vile veggies clung momentarily to the ceiling before eventually scattering like a rain shower over the room.

The only thing that survived the tumultuous spill was the Jell-O salad, which miraculously remained suctioned to my plate.

Unfortunately, my siblings and cousins were also victims of the flying food shrapnel.

Everyone burst into laughter. That was, everyone except me. Not because I was hurt or had just lost my Christmas dinner. I knew there was plenty more food available, even those repulsive veggies, and I wouldn't go hungry.

However, the problem that made me shudder even thinking about it was my mom never understood our graceless kid accidents. I was terrified of facing her in my scattered, covered, and smothered state.

Once the laughter subsided and the scene was fully assessed, the reality settled. All the other kids also knew Mom was not the most compassionate or patient adult, so a plan was quickly devised.

One of my cousins would go upstairs and ask their mom—my aunt—to come down. We would explain the situation and get her help clean-up. We knew because of an ongoing feud between my mom and her that my aunt would be our strongest ally.

The plan was set into action and soon my aunt appeared. She took one look at the mess, saw my apprehensive face, and rushed over to me.

Rather than receiving a scolding about being careful and how much of a mess I'd made, my aunt misjudged the situation.

She smiled and asked in a kind, solemn voice, "Oh, honey... did you throw up?"

That brought a whole new round of laughter and much relief to me.

She quickly cleaned up the food and even went and got me a new plate without my mom knowing and *without* vegetables.

In the end, I concluded that a dinner without veggies was worth all the dried gravy, potatoes, and everything else I had to painstakingly get combed out of my hair later. I couldn't remember how I even explained the mess to my mom. I don't even think I got scolding for it.

I guess the gods smiled down on me that Christmas.

Chapter 18

Our Most Memorable Christmas Ever

Elsabe Botha

December 1987
Roodekrans, South Africa

O ur *son, Reinhart,* was five and our daughter, Roelien, was two when we had our most memorable Christmas ever.

At the time, we lived in Roodekrans, a suburb of Johannesburg, South Africa. This was the third Christmas in a row we'd celebrated at this house. The tree stood in the same place every year; a corner of our sitting room.

Reinhart wrote letters to Father Christmas on behalf of his sister and himself every year. It was a very detailed letter (which he dictated to me and I wrote), to make sure Father Christmas would find his way not only to our house, but right to the tree inside:

"Father Christmas, when you enter the front door, turn left and then turn right. You will see the Christmas tree right in front of you."

Roelien did her part, too. She put a small lamp on the table next to the tree so Father Christmas would not fall over anything on his way to the tree. The brother and sister team made sure Father Christmas would not get lost and be safe doing it.

This specific December, we decided on a whim to celebrate Christmas with my sister, Sonja, and her husband, Chris, at the Vaal River where we owned a piece of land. Since Christmas in South Africa was actually during summer vacation, it often rained and stormed on Christmas Eve and Christmas day.

We always went to the Vaal River in our trailer. It was big with enough space for eight people to sleep comfortably. This year, however, we wanted even more room, so Sonja, Chris, my husband, Butch, and I, decided to split the cost and buy a huge tent we could attach to the trailer. This way, we would be able to put a table and chairs in it and have our dinner in style and put up a Christmas tree for the children.

We packed up everything in our car and trailer and drove to our destination. We were on the road for about forty minutes when Reinhart cried out in a devastated sounding voice.

"We have big problems, Mom."

I turned around in my seat and looked at him with concern. "What's wrong?"

"Remember, Mom? We wrote to Father Christmas. We told him we would be home. Now we won't. We'll be at the river."

Butch and I glanced at each other and he pulled off the road at the next gas station so we could make a call at a phone booth (no cell-phones back then), to Father Christmas. He left his door open so the children could hear everything. They watched with big eyes as he explained our situation.

"Hi, Santa! I just want to let you know we will not be at our house for Christmas. We will be at the Vaal River. Uh-huh… yes. The Christmas tree will be in the tent. Thank you, Father Christmas."

Our children did not seem to be convinced Father Christmas would find his way, but we assured them everything would be okay.

When we finally arrived at the river, we started putting up the tent. Chris and Sonja arrived twenty minutes later with the gifts for the children stashed in the trunk of their car.

It was Christmas Eve and we were set. The tent was attached to the trailer with the chairs, table, and tree set up. Everything looked good. All that remained for us to do was to get the presents from Sonja and Chris's car and put them under the tree.

The car was parked up on the hill, but getting the gifts out was more difficult than one might think. The children were watching the goings-on with interest. We simply couldn't find a gap to go and get the presents without them noticing.

Then, a storm started brewing. Thunder clapped loudly and lightning flashed. It started raining hard and the wind swirled like crazy. The rain began coming down in torrents. Chris and Butch grabbed spades and started digging trenches to guide the building water away from the tent and trailer. The wind picked up even more and Sonja, Reinhart, and I were forced to hold onto the tent poles to keep the whole thing from blowing away.

While Reinhart held onto the pole with all his might, he screamed out. "There is no way Father Christmas will bring presents in this storm."

Sonja and I looked at each other thinking the same thing.

How are we going to get the darn presents from their car, high up that hill, in this *torrential rain?*

Climbing that hill through the mud wouldn't be possible.

Roelien asked hopefully, "Can we take boots and a raincoat to Father Christmas?"

The idea was one of us would go to the car, get presents, and put them under the tree in the tent. As usual, that person would ring a bell after placing the presents under the tree, which would be the sign to the children that Santa and his sleigh had left the building and their

This simple plan seemed impossible.

No one wanted to do this. We had to draw straws to decide who was going to run through rain, lightning, and thunder up the muddy hill.

Chris was the unlucky one.

I went into the trailer and Chris went around the back. I was to secretly hand him the bell. When I stuck my hand, with the bell, through the window, Chris reached for it, but he slid in the mud and fell.

The bell rang.

Chaos erupted.

Children screamed and ran around like mad chickens, yelling, "Father Christmas came! Father Christmas came! Our presents are here!"

Reinhart let go of the pole he was still holding onto. The kids made a bee-line for the trailer from where the sound of the bell was coming. When they ran into the bedroom, I rolled off the bed onto the floor, away from the window, and motioned to the kids.

"I'm hiding from Father Christmas. He doesn't like it when people see him deliver presents."

They promptly fell to the ground like obedient soldiers, doing the leopard crawl toward me.

"We should stay right here and be quiet or else Santa might turn around and leave with your presents."

The kids nodded vigorously with big eyes.

"I'm going to close the door, okay?" I said.

I didn't want the children to see Chris when he brought in the presents.

Still on the floor, I snuck to the door, hoping Chris was back. Sonja and Butch, who were still holding onto tent poles, stared down at me, frowning.

"What *are* you doing?" they asked simultaneously.

"I don't know," I said, as I stood up and brushed my pants down.

Sonja said, "Everything is okay. The presents are under the tree."

I heard a shuffling, peered up, and I stifled a scream. There, in the tent, stood an enormous mud monster. It was Chris covered in sludge from head to toe. Muck was literally dripping from him and he shook from being extremely cold and wet through to his skin. He must have slipped and slid a lot as he crawled up that muddy hill.

Reinhart and Roelien came out of the trailer and saw poor, shivering Chris.

"Where were you, Uncle Chris?" Reinhart asked insistently. "You missed Father Christmas. He was here just now. I wonder if he is also covered in mud like you are."

Sonja wrapped a blanket around her husband and tried wiping his face with a paper towel.

The wind started blowing more than ever and we grabbed onto the tent poles again.

The rest of the night played off like this: When a person's name was read off, to receive his/her present, he had to quickly let go of the pole, run and get the present, and then run back again to grab the pole again.

Later, we grownups sat on chairs next to our pole, holding onto it with one hand and eating our Christmas dinner with the other.

Although it might be considered to be miserably bad and the absolute worst, Christmas, working together as a family, we made it work and it was, without a doubt, our most memorable Christmas ever.

Chapter

19

The Unwanted Christmas Tree

Alecia Drake

December 1977
Ogden, Utah

Most Christmases during my childhood were filled with excitement and expectation. We would wake up before the sun rose to find assembled racetracks plugged in and ready to go and remote controlled toys fully charged, begging to chase the dog. They'd flip over and roll down the stairs never to operate again.

My upbringing was loaded with this polarity, moments that began picture perfect only to unravel into some totally bizarre, unexpected series of completely inappropriate emotional states that never concluded into anything constructive.

As a child, I didn't fully understand the relationship between my father and stepmother. They both had a tendency to be very potent, always right, arguing often just to represent a different view than the other. These arguments could get wild, loud, and, quite frankly, dangerous if you were a kid. Being in the crossfire of a debate gone bad could land you into a multitude of undesirable outcomes.

One such discussion began regarding taking down the Christmas tree. We always had a real tree, so taking it down required some effort. First, the ornaments had to be removed and repackaged. Next, each string of lights was unraveled from the branches while needles fell on the floor. Then, we'd pick up the tree and carry it out the front door with a carpet of needles trailing behind.

This specific year, a couple days after Christmas, my stepmom requested my father to take down the tree.

The requests went something like this...

"Will you take down the tree?"

No response. I suspected Dad was sleeping on the couch and if he could hear her, he was not going to acknowledge it.

"John, will you put the tree away?"

Grunt, roll over, and back to snoring.

"Are you going to take the f*cking tree down?"

Okay, now things were heating up. This was the queue to leave the room, which I promptly did.

Over the course of twenty minutes, I heard two or so more iterations of her request to my father, whom I assumed was still horizontal.

However, I jumped from a horrible crashing sound in the living room. Not sure what happened, I ran downstairs only to see my stepmom or, more accurately, her arm trying to maneuver our "f*cking Christmas tree."

She wasn't particularly nimble with the tree and, at first, I wasn't sure what the hell she was doing. The expletives kept flowing and my dad decided it was best he keep on sleeping.

My brother and I watched our stepmom over the course of several minutes as she managed to knock over the still-decorated tree, open the front door, and pick it back up only to be halted by the light cords. With a deft yank, she freed the cords and picked the tree back up and headed for the open door. However, the tree didn't easily fit. Decorations crashed and skittered across the floor as she put her whole weight behind it.

On the third attempt, the tree shot through the door in a symphony of crunching lights and ornaments. The bulk first landed on the front porch and my stepmom fell on top of it. She stood up and with one more effort, she hefted the tree and thrust it off the porch to its final resting place in our front yard.

She turned around appearing extremely satisfied and didn't look back, not even once. She walked in the front door, slammed it, shaking the house, and stormed off to her bedroom.

Dad didn't move.

(I couldn't blame him.)

That was where our tree landed and where it remained.

The tree radiated Christmas joy from my front yard for all to see until that spring. Most mornings, my bus ride began with Jingle Bells, even after the snow melted.

To this day, I can't remember who finally broke down and picked the tree up and took care of it.

I'd be willing to bet good money it wasn't my stepmom.

Chapter

20

We Wish You a Merry Keys-mas

Marley Gibson

December 2011
Marathon, Florida Keys

M y husband, Patrick, and I are what you'd call an "encore couple" which meant the bride and groom were both previously married, but had found love again. By definition, *encore* means "a second achievement that especially surpasses the first."

That was certainly the case with us.

We knew this time around, marriage was going to be much different, so we wanted to make it memorable, unique, and adventurous.

Our first step toward this was purchasing a thirty-four foot, class A, RV motorhome—we affectionately referred to as Midge—and putting most of our belongings in storage in order to live on the road and travel the country from coast to coast. Our adventures took us to the bottom of the Grand Canyon in a helicopter, paragliding over Destin, on the deck of the *Maid of the Mist II* getting drenched under Niagara Falls, and visiting the Big Peach, the Space Acorn, and the Very Large Array. In particular, we got married on 11/11/11 at 11:11 a.m. in the Florida Keys...

...in Key Largo's John Pennekamp Coral Reef State Park.

...off a boat.

...at the Christ of the Abyss eight and a half-foot bronze statue.

...twenty-five feet underwater.

Yes, a SCUBA wedding.

See, we'd both done our first weddings the "traditional" way and we saw how those turned out. This time, we planned the adventurous, encore celebration to represent our exciting new life together. (Or, as my mother called it, "the kooky ceremony.")

No matter, we have enjoyed this mid-life revival living and learning from each other and traveling far and wide.

After the wedding, we decided to park Midge for a while in an RV park in Marathon, Florida— the midway point in the Florida Keys. The park was filled with fifth wheels, tie downs, and other motorhomes.

My husband grew up in Chicago and I was from Boston, so a Caribbean-like holiday season was something neither one of us was familiar with. We enjoyed snorkeling for lobsters, fishing off the back pier of the resort, and swimming in the heated pool. But, that spirit of Christmas simply wasn't in the air.

There were no evergreens or Fraser firs. No greenery hanging anywhere or wreathes bearing holly and pine cones. The decorations were more beach-themed and reflective of the area. In fact, a bank on US 1 in Marathon had a lawn display with Santa in a sled being pulled by sunglass-wearing dolphins. It wasn't the traditional Yule log on the fire while drinking hot chocolate and wearing slippers in front of the family tree while singing carols.

We had each other and our new life.

However, we needed to get into the holiday spirit even though the white stuff surrounding us was sand instead of snow. Regardless of being over sixteen hours away from our closest relative, we were determined not to be bah humbug-y and accept the Keys' way of Christmas.

Since we'd just paid for a wedding, we didn't have funds to go overboard for presents and such. And, because our closest family and friends had recently bought us wedding gifts, we couldn't expect them to turn around and give us any more. There probably wasn't going to be anything to open on Christmas morning and there certainly wouldn't be the delicious smells of the season coming from my mother's or Patrick's father's kitchens. The golden turkey, the tangy cranberry sauce, buttery mashed potatoes, onion and celery-laced dressing, glazed ham, pineapple and green bean casseroles, and so many desserts you'd pop a button simply looking at them.

We decided we'd lay low, live off the land (crab, shrimp, fish, and lobster), and let Christmas come and go on its own.

It wasn't that easy, though.

Christmas had always been a special time of year for me. I was born on December 28th and grew up with a great big, colorfully lit, shiny, decorated tree that stayed up for my birthday. This year, though, my homemade ornaments and decorations were in a storage locker north of Atlanta. No garland or lights. No advent calendar or tree skirt. Just palm trees, iguanas, and ocean breezes.

One day while we were out and about, we ended up at this kitschy dime store place that also sold hero sandwiches, bait, and fishing gear. All the things we Conchs needed on a daily basis. While waiting for our lunch to be made, we rummaged throughout the aisle of cheap, touristy things. They had Christmas decorations out; mostly ornaments bedecked with various fish, seashells, seahorses, anchors, ship's wheels, sand dollars, and starfish. For only a handful of money, we picked up several seasonal adornments to scatter throughout the rig and try to capture the holiday spirit.

Patrick had some strings of LED lights underneath the rig that had been given to us for trimming our awning when parked. We thought stringing them around the palm tree in our camping slot would be fun and add to the overall atmosphere. We hung the ornaments from the palm tree, as well, to add to our festive attempts.

There was just one more thing...

Friends of ours had given us a lawn zombie as a pre-wedding present. (Don't ask or judge...) It was one of those half-humans appearing as if it were crawling out of the ground. Something you purchased out of a Sky Mall catalog. Something sooooooo us.

We'd named him Bob—again, don't ask—and always set him out whenever we parked the rig for a while. So, Patrick put Santa hat on Bob and we stuck a candy cane in his curled zombie hand.

For anyone who has ever stayed in an RV camp, you know there are a lot of older people in residence at any given time. In this case, they were mostly snowbirds from Michigan, Minnesota, New Hampshire, and Canada. They drove their golf carts on the resort roads and didn't like anything out of the norm from their set vacation world.

Bob was certainly *not* something any of them had seen before. They'd slow their golf carts down in front of our rig and stare at the zombie, pointing and scowling at him.

This happened every day. All day long. The parade of golf carts and other vehicles slowing to a creepy-crawl to gawk at Bob. Patrick found it hilarious, but I was starting to feel as if we didn't belong. It was bad enough we were forty-years younger than most of the other people, but now we'd gone and put a big, red target on ourselves by placing our Santa-fied zombie out front.

Was this going to be the worst Christmas ever? How could it be? We were newlyweds. We wanted it to be perfect.

On Christmas Eve, however, we saw a flyer posted at the shower houses announcing there would be a resort-wide Christmas dinner at the pavilion, down by the pier. Ham and turkey would be provided by the resort, but they asked residents in attendance to please bring a side dish or dessert to share. We would also need to bring our own plates and silverware.

We thought about it and decided it was a great option to have some traditional holiday food—not just seafood—but it would mean we'd have to sit around with the judgmental old people who constantly stopped and stared at our slot. Perhaps, we could simply slip in, eat, say "Thanks" and "Merry Christmas," and scoot out.

I needed to bring a side dish, though.

What would please a varied crowd like this? I didn't have a lot in my pantry because we'd been eating out a lot. And, we hadn't purchased the traditional seasonal food to prepare for ourselves. The only thing I thought to bring was deviled eggs. I could make a lot of them—enough for many to share—and I had garnered accolades for them over the years.

Egg-cellent. That would work.

So, I made two dozen deviled eggs with my not-so-secret recipe (mayo, salt, pepper, spicy mustard, and paprika) and on Christmas day around noon, Patrick and I set off to the pavilion at the back of the resort.

When we got there, people were already lined up with various dinnerware in hand, ready for the resort manager to start carving the bird. There were casseroles of all sorts and varieties, potatoes that were mashed, baked, and roasted. Numerous bowls of salads of the seafood, chicken, and pasta varieties, overflowing with large serving spoons. Rolls, cranberry sauce, and stuffings sat nearby in large throw-away aluminum roasting pans. There was a veritable smorgasbord of food – something for everyone.

I felt good setting down my large tray of deviled eggs until I saw… another platter of deviled eggs nearby. They'd apparently been made by a woman named Lillian who was a popular and regular visitor to the resort.

Oh great… here I am trying to show her up.

After a blessing was given and we all said, "Amen," the line shifted quickly and the food began to disappear before our eyes as hungry older people piled a bit of everything onto their plate. I noticed most people went straight to Lillian's deviled eggs. Sure, a few individuals took mine, as well, but her tray cleared off immediately. I snagged one of them to see what the big deal was with her version.

I skulked back to the rear of the pavilion and sat next to Patrick who was heartily enjoying his Christmas lunch. I picked up Lillian's deviled egg and took a bite… and swiftly reached for my napkin to spit it out.

I wasn't sure exactly what was wrong with it, but it was… *nasty.* She'd dowsed it with way too much mayonnaise salt, curry powder, and what I could only define as a heaping helping of cayenne pepper. I normally enjoyed such tastes, but together in this egg filling, it was totally wrong on so many levels.

Apparently, I wasn't the only one who thought the same way.

I noticed many others setting Lillian's eggs to the side of their plate. And, as the meal went along, I saw folks get up, return to the buffet table, and snag *my* deviled eggs. One by one, my treats began to disappear as people nudged each other, pointed, and more eggs were taken and eaten. Before I knew it, they were all gone.

One man went up to the table and asked, "What happened to the good eggs?"

Another woman said, "Those were the best deviled eggs I've ever had."

An older, white-haired woman laughed heartily and said, "I guess mine weren't the big hit this year. Sorry. Those—" she said, pointing to my tray, "—are *much* better."

Someone else chimed in, "You've met your match, Lillian."

Oh crap! That *is Lillian?*

"Who made these?" Lillian asked.

Patrick, oblivious to the food fight going down, nudged me and then said, "My wife did."

I know I must have blushed from head to toe when every eye in the place fell on us in what I could only interpret as scrutinized judgment. We weren't regulars. We weren't snowbirds. We weren't true Conchs. We were outsiders who'd invaded their celebration and now I'd gone and shown up the matron of the yearly Christmas dinner.

"You made them?" asked a woman. I recognized her as the lady who lived across the street from us in the resort.

I swallowed hard. "Yes, ma'am."

She smiled broadly. "They're *delicious!*"

138

"They are," Lillian agreed.

I let out the breath I'd been holding. They weren't annoyed or mad. They weren't judging or hating. They actually liked my food.

Then, the man who'd been standing at the egg tray lowered his brows and stared right at us. "Aren't y'all the ones with the yard zombie?"

My eyes widened and my heart started racing like a speedboat. Now, we were going to get it. The weirdoes with the lawn zombie poking fun at their holiday celebration.

"Yeah, that's us," Patrick said.

Several people started laughing and one guy said, "I love that thing!"

"Me too," someone echoed.

Lillian clapped her hands. "My grandkids posed with it the other day for a picture. I hope that was okay."

"Sure," I said, relaxing. "That's hilarious."

"We're going to get our picture made after we finish eating," another person said.

Patrick elbowed me again. "How about that? Bob is popular."

He was… and so were we.

A bunch of people visited that afternoon, snapping selfies with Bob, some even laying on the ground to pose with him. One lady had her dog photographed with him.

As the sun set and our lights twinkled brightly, Patrick and I walked together hand-in-hand down to the pier and stood at the water's edge glancing up at the magnificent and expansive sky painted with stars and planets sparkling back.

It wasn't anything like a traditional Christmas celebration—kooky, in fact—but it was perfect for us. For our crazy, adventurous, fun-filled, and encore life together.

Merry Keys-mas to all and to all, a good night.

Chapter

21

The Blackened Turkey

Rebecca Ory Hernandez

December 1977
South Louisiana

I t was a typical Christmas Day in South Louisiana. The year was 1977 and the air was cooler than usual, around seventy degrees and not quite warm enough to utilize the air conditioner.

Mom always worked for at least two weeks prior to Christmas preparing special dishes she only cooked for Christmas dinner. The oven was cranking out casseroles, side dishes, and dinner rolls. We kids would beg for a taste or a snack. She'd shoo us outside to play with our cousins so we wouldn't be under her feet in the kitchen.

We had a lot of people at our house for the holiday celebrations—both sides of the family. They could hardly fit in our ranch-style bungalow that normally sat four at the dinner table. Now, there were wooden table extensions to pull out of storage from the coat closet to accommodate the extra bodies, as well as a child's table set up for the four little ones. The older kids got to eat at the bar counter. This was carefully orchestrated so when the turkey was ready everyone would stand around to say grace. The turkey would be carved and dinner would be devoured in less than an hour.

This particular year, we were having something new – a *smoked* turkey. Dad had gotten a new smoker as a Christmas gift and couldn't wait to use it. Why Mom allowed this, we'll never know, but when Dad had set his mind to do something, that was the way it was going to be. I remember hearing him tell my uncle he started the turkey at 4:00 a.m. Dinner was usually served around 1:00 p.m. For an eight-year-old girl, that seemed awfully early to me.

We kids were playing in the backyard and the adults were scattered about on the patio and in the den, puffing away on cigarettes and having pre-dinner cocktails. The kitchen was abuzz with activity; the ladies warming up the side dishes and chatting away on every subject. Their husbands gathered outside telling stories about college football and hunting conquests. The radio outside blared Christmas songs and the TV inside was tuned to a football game.

Finally, everything was turned off and it became silent when Dad proudly walked in with the turkey on a fancy platter and announced it was time to eat.

But, there was a problem.

A fifteen-pound problem.

The turkey was smoked all right, but it wasn't the beautiful golden brown we'd expected,
It was charbroiled to a sooty black.

At that point, Mom yelled, "What have you done? It's burned! What will people eat?" Her rant was followed by flowing tears.

My grandmother consoled her, "*Mais chez*, we have lots of food to eat. Look at all this other food. No one will go hungry today."

However, Mom wouldn't have it. She went on and on about the turkey being blackened to a crisp and what was she going to serve everyone.

I ran around to the other side of the counter to watch from a safe distance—someone was going to get it for sure.

Without a word, Dad peeled back the layers of charred skin, set it aside, took the electric knife, and carved the bird into perfect slices. No problem. Just like any other holiday.

And, there it was.

The inside was perfectly cooked and juicy.

In fact, it was one of the best turkeys we'd ever eater.

And as such, it became our family tradition to have smoked turkey along with ham every Christmas.

Blackened or not.

Chapter

22

Batteries Not Included

Elsabe Botha

December 1985
Sandton, South Africa

It was time for the Christmas party at my office.

I worked at a branch of Rand Merchant Bank, in Sandton, Johannesburg. The party was held in a park close to the office and was for office workers' children and organized by three wonderful women, Amanda, Elna, and Bets. They always did a great job with this event and Burger, our branch manager, loved playing Santa.

The parents bought the presents and dropped them off at the office where they were wrapped and ready for Santa who would give them to the children.

Our son, Reinhart, was four years old that year. He really wanted a remote-controlled truck. He could hardly wait or hold in his excitement as we drove through the midday traffic from De Deur, our suburb on the outskirts of

Johannesburg, into Sandton, where I worked.

It was a very hot day, which was usual in South Africa since December was in the middle of summer. Treats were served at the party before Santa arrived, but Reinhart did not eat a thing. He was too anxious and kept on glancing around, first at the tree where an enormous pile of presents waited, then at the empty throne-like chair where Santa would sit, and finally, to the gate where Santa would enter... and back to the presents again.

At last, the children and parents were asked to sit in the chairs lined up in front of the tree. Soon enough, we heard bells followed by a ho-ho-ho. Santa bounded through the gate and sat down in his chair. The children were super quiet and stared at him with big eyes.

Father Christmas's helper asked the children to line up and told them when Father Christmas called their names, they should walk up to him to get their present.

I felt sorry for the kids standing in that long line on this extremely hot day, but they did not seem to mind.

"Reinhart Botha," Father Christmas called out. Reinhart walked up and climbed upon Santa's lap.

I was close enough to hear Santa say, "You must have been a very good boy because look at this big present."

Reinhart was overcome with awe and said, "Thank you, Father Christmas."

He hopped off his lap and walked off seeming quite pleased. He immediately tore into the box as he walked toward us. A huge smile broke out over his face. He sat down right there and took the truck out to admire it.

After a moment, though, he frowned, got up, turned around, and walked back to the line where children were still waiting to see Father Christmas.

I went over to Reinhart, "What are you doing, sweetie?"

"There are no batteries, Mom. I am going to ask him about them. He must have forgotten to put it in the box."

"Oh, sweetie, I'll buy batteries for the truck."

He shook his head firmly and continued to wait in line in the blazing heat until the rest of the kids received their presents. Reinhart climbed back into Father Christmas's lap again.

"So, son," the bearded man said, "You already have your present. Did you come back to thank me?"

Reinhart said, "No, Father Christmas. There aren't any batteries in the box. I think you must still have it in your pocket."

Father Christmas smiled and said, "Son, unfortunately, I ran out. Can you do me a huge favor? Please ask your mother to go to the store and buy some. It will really help out."

Reinhart smiled broadly, nodded, and jumped off his lap and ran toward us.

Apparently, he had to hear it from Santa himself.

150

Chapter

23

A Christmas Quandary

Erica Hattingh-Smith

December 2014
Tauranga, New Zealand

I live in a harbor-side city in the Bay of Plenty, on New Zealand's North Island. A bridge over the harbor connects Tauranga to Mount Maunganui, a beach town.

Three years ago, I took my four-year-old grandson, Ezra, to see Christmas lights on Plover Avenue, a cul-de-sac in Maungatapu. The homeowners there spent weeks, perhaps even months, decorating their homes and gardens for the season. Properties were bedecked in fairy lights to brighten the night as part of the tradition. The homeowners also put treats out in front of their houses for visitors.

It really was a wonderland full of Christmas spirit. They even had a Father Christmas every year. The street's lights were an established attraction on the "Weekend Sun's Christmas Lights Trails."

This event was known far and wide and people came from all over to experience this quaint celebration. It was a tradition for me taking my grandsons there every year.

A couple days before Christmas, I was babysitting Ezra because my daughter was working. Walking into the street while holding my grandson's hand, I felt the festive lights and decorations were even more beautiful than I remembered. Every single house was adorned and the street looked cheerful and bright. There were so many people milling about, walking up and down the street and on the sidewalks—the atmosphere was exciting and jovial. People stopped and talked to each other, wishing each other a Merry Christmas.

Ezra was in his element. He was so excited to meet Father Christmas who sat in a chair in front of one of the houses. Ezra asked him all types of questions and they had a great conversation.

We continued our walk through the Christmas wonderland. An older lady stopped us and asked Ezra, "Does your house have a chimney, little boy? You know Father Christmas delivers the presents that way, right?"

Ezra looked up at the old lady and look concerned, "I don't know," he said with innocence written all over his face.

I saw the doubt creep across his face and it pulled at my heartstrings. I don't think he ever had reason to see if his house had a chimney or not. Now, it was of paramount concern to him.

When we arrived back at my house, Ezra instantly wanted me to call his mother.

He took my cell phone from me, put it on speaker, and asked in his worried little voice, "Mom, does our house have a chimney?"

"No, we don't," she told him honestly.

He swallowed hard and asked, "Mom, do you think it will be okay if we leave the front door open for Father Christmas?"

A smile broke over his face as he listened to his mother's response.

"I suppose we can do that."

"Bye, Mom!"

With this quandary solved, Ezra climbed into bed and slept like a rock, knowing his Christmas would be just fine.

Chapter

24

A Fiery Christmas

Rebecca Hernandez

Christmas Eve 1980
Gramercy, Louisiana

It was one holiday I'd never forget.

We had houseguests, as we always did, and after our traditional gumbo supper, we took a ride along River Road to see the bonfires lighting the way for Papa Noel before returning home to shoot off fireworks.

I was a sullen fifteen-year-old, as are most fifteen-year-olds, and I wasn't really excited about Christmas that particular year.

I mean, what was the big deal?

Sure, we had a had a house full of guests, friends, family, and neighbors - a big open house from 6:00-10:00 p.m. as did most Cajun families. And as was tradition, after the gumbo supper, we took a ride along River Road to see the bonfires that lit the way for Papa Noel.

This was a really big fete, but I wasn't in the mood for the same old same old same old

Christmas Eve blah, blah, blah boring tradition. I wanted snow or something exciting to happen. And, I felt as though there was nothing that year that would make me happy since I didn't have a boyfriend or girlfriend or anyone other than the same old people I saw every year doing the same old bad jokes and drinking the same old highballs after dinner.

After getting our fill of community fireworks, we would all return home where the kids would do small fireworks as entertainment to stay out of the adults' festivities.

The town I grew up in was small, and lucky for us, across the street from my house was a large baseball park. There were three diamonds which translated to lots and lots of grass. A field was nearly a city block.

That year, the grass was extra dry due to a lack of rainfall in December. I tagged along with my sister and a couple of newly made friends of a business acquaintance of my dad's. There were only four of us and we went about the business of the boring, traditional, small-scale fireworks: basic firecrackers, innocent sparklers, and something we'd not lit before called "jumping jacks."

I wasn't thrilled. I remember thinking, "I'm cold and there's no snow and there's nothing to do but stand out here freezing and hanging out with children?"

We were on the pitcher's mound lighting one or two small firecrackers at a time and I was having none of that. I decided I might as well light an entire pack of jumping jacks to see what might happen. I thought this was a marvelous idea. I mean, what was the worst thing that could happen? It might improve this dreaded same old same old. It seemed harmless enough.

So, I lit the fuse of the pack which was bound tightly together and the fireworks danced in several different directions popping and crackling. We all ran in different directions laughing as the jumping jacks did some mini explosions.

It was finally getting fun until part of the outfield caught fire. Then, it spread quickly to the opposite end of the field before we could even blink. We tried putting out a small patch of dry grass by stomping on it like we'd been taught at school and it seemed to work, only to jump to another patch, then another and another until I'd never seen flames as high as those before.

I was scared to death of what my father might do, much less the Fire Marshall whom everyone in town knew was busy with the bonfires at the levee. If my father knew I was part of something that caused such destruction to our beautiful neighborhood park... well, I didn't want to think about it.

Neighbors and friends arrived from several directions with buckets of ice and water from their parties to try to douse the flames, but it kept getting out of control. By the time the water hose from one of the other neighbors on the opposite corner who had heard our screams for help extinguished the flames, we'd scorched the entire outfield.

Neither our parents nor the fire department knew what had happened because everyone was occupied with their parties and festivities, never suspecting the "good kids" from across the park would be burning the baseball field. No one noticed until Christmas Day when the sun came out, exposing a field of charred grass.

As I looked out the living room window from the safety of my home, it struck me funny that I'd finally had a good Christmas filled with new excitement I could never have anticipated.

I gazed out at the blackened field when I witnessed another family do the same thing I'd done the night before. They must have thought it was a good idea to pop fireworks at the park. Of course, parts of the outfield not already singed, caught on fire on Christmas Day.

My sister and I laughed remembering the excitement from the night before.

Who said family fireworks were boring?

Why... they could make for one of the best Christmas memories ever.

(Note: No one is allowed to use explosives in the park any longer. For obvious reasons.)

Chapter 25

The Best Worst Christmas Ever

Lynda Scott

December 1939
Utah

This dilapidated, shabby cabin was what life had come to for Hilda and her children. The Great Depression, which began a decade ago, still raged in 1939.

Since no one had extra money for piano lessons, Hilda had lost students one-by-one until she had only two of them remaining paying ten cents a week each. Most men couldn't find jobs and there weren't any for women. Not even the children's father, Clay, who had left their family a year ago, had been able to provide support for the kids. How could Hilda feed four children between the ages of seven and thirteen on twenty cents a week?

Desperation drove her to the only option available. She needed to rent out her house in the city and move to this old cabin on her father's property. At least, it provided a roof over their heads and, most importantly, their needs would be met.

Now, resistant legs held Hilda in the doorway unable to enter the cabin, which until last week had housed farm equipment. The items had been removed, a path to the front door was cleared through the tumbleweeds, and a broken window was replaced.

The utter and complete dinginess and dirtiness of the place sent waves of nausea through her. How could they live here? Yes, many would think any roof over your head as luxurious, but it brought shame to Hilda, and apparently to Dorothy, her oldest daughter.

The girl leaned against the car with her arms folded across her chest and her head down. What facial features of hers Hilda could see were riddled with anguish as tears spilled into the dirt at Dorothy's feet. Hilda jangled the car keys in her pocket for assurance that her daughter could not escape back to the city.

Hilda rallied the kids and began making the cabin into a home. They brought in buckets of water from the creek, washed walls and windows, swept floors, mended fences for a garden, chopped wood for the stove, hung curtains, set up the furniture they had brought with them, and the made beds.

Her sons, Paul and Jesse had beds set up in the attic despite the low ceilings. The kitchen table and chairs filled a corner of the cooking area and one bed for Dorothy and her youngest daughter, Betty, to share, and one for Hilda, filled the remainder of the downstairs.

The previous week, each child had been provided with one box to move with them and several to pack and leave at the house. Packing had no sooner started before Hilda heard what she'd expected.

"Seriously, Mother. One box won't hold even half of what I need to take." It was Dorothy, of course. Now, as they unpacked those boxes, the lack of space became woefully apparent.

Dinner had never tasted as good as when they'd assembled around the table that evening. The children ate in silence, tiredness obvious on their faces. They had made a good start and tomorrow promised more improvements.

After the kids fell asleep, Hilda brewed a pot of tea and clasped the warm cup in her hands against the coolness of the high-country night air. Tiredness cricked every muscle in her body while she unpacked the kitchen boxes and put away as much as space allowed. She rubbed her forehead and glanced around the diminutive space. She added shelving material to her growing list of needed items.

Sun beaming through the kitchen window the next morning shone directly on Hilda. She reluctantly threw back her covers and went to the stove and put water on to heat. Before it reached a boil, all four kids surrounded her, threatening to eat anything in sight.

"Dorothy, you make the best oatmeal. How about cooking our very first breakfast?"

Dorothy shot her a frown, but reached for the oats.

How do you tear a thirteen-year-year-old away from the only home she's known, away from her teenage friends, and expect her to be happy in the country?

It would be a battle every day.

In time, new shelves lined the kitchen walls, more hooks hung clothing for five people, a chicken coop had been built and filled with a hen donated from each of their neighbors, and a garden had been planted. Soon, green beans and tomatoes sprouted, pumpkin vines wended their way around potato hills, and squash grew abundantly. Hilda had brought flower seeds with her and blue-violet Morning Glory adorned the fence around the garden; mint, marigolds and the hens helped keep the bugs at bay, and color and fragrance filled the yard. Hilda could almost be happy; at least her children seemed to be.

Within days of their move, country kids had ventured into the yard. They were rewarded by samples of Betty's fudge. The kids' new friends showed them the best fishing holes, where to find berries—which Hilda made into pies—how to trap gophers and catch frogs, how to pull pitch from pine trees for gum, and at least a hundred other things. Even Dorothy made friends and began to smile more.

To her delight, people asked Hilda to play the piano for church dances. It didn't pay much, but Hilda socked it away for Christmas. Farm life was tough and winters here could be brutal. A special Christmas would help keep the kids from hitchhiking back to the city.

December snows made life difficult on the farm and the kids pleaded loudly to move back to the city. At the cabin, nobody came to clear snow from the dirt roads. No indoor plumbing meant slop jars or freezing trips to the outhouse. Hilda vowed to find a way to make this the best Christmas yet and do everything in her power to create a positive memory of their time at the farm.

She'd warned the kids Christmas would be bleak without money for presents and no room in the house for a tree. There also would be no party at their dad's work where Santa visited and each child received a stocking filled with small candies, nuts, a few pennies, and a real orange. The kids' gasps filled the air when Hilda told them about not going to the party.

"Mother, I don't want to live here anymore," seven-year-old Jesse wailed. "I want an orange."

Unanimous responses resounded. "Me too."

Hilda gathered them around her and fought to restrain tears. "Do you remember the book we read about the boxcar children?"

A nod of heads answered, except for Dorothy, who most likely thought the book too childish for her.

Hilda continued, "Sometimes we have to go through hardships in life. I wish it weren't like this or that you had a kind, wealthy grandfather to come rescue you like the boxcar children, but we're more fortunate than many people by having our boxcar cabin."

"My friend, Mary's family lost their home and had to go live in a dirt basement. Mary said they fixed it up with wood floors and walls, but her dad couldn't stand up straight because the ceiling was too short. I hate The Depression," Betty said.

"Me too, darling. But let's do what we can to create a bright Christmas. How about making cards for your friends and for a child in the orphanage in the city?'

"Are we going to do gifts for each other again this year?" Paul asked. He and Dorothy were the quietest of the four, so it surprised Hilda for him to ask. Perhaps it was due to dread, not interest.

Soon decorations accumulated, cards were mailed, and the children found or made a gift for each sibling. The kids cut out snowflakes from the Montgomery Ward catalog and hung them from string to circle the living room. It was beginning to look like Christmas.

With the children at school during the day, Hilda set her secret plans in motion, thanks to her savings. She picked up the fabric from the general store she had been paying on a bit at a time and began sewing new clothes for the kids. At the end of each day, she hid her work in the trunk of the car because Betty found everything in the tiny cabin.

However, the oranges plagued her. The kids really looked forward to them every year and the ones in town were expensive and old. Maybe her cousin, Henry, who worked on the train, could find some in the city.

A few days before Christmas, the clothes were finished, hair barrettes matching the girls' dresses had been purchased, and a small gift for every child from "Santa" had been wrapped. Candles, sequins, and other items for decorating, as well as food for a delightful Christmas dinner, had been purchased and hidden. Most of all, the oranges had arrived. Four beautiful, big ones.

The Christmas tree remained Hilda's only concern. Plenty of juniper trees dotted the valley and a few pines could be found in the snow-covered hills, but unless she cut off only the very top, any tree would be too large for their tiny cabin.

An idea captivated Hilda and she set to work on her surprise. It might backfire and send the kids fleeing to the city, but she had to do something besides the oranges to make this holiday memorable.

On Christmas morning, Hilda rose before the cock began to crow and built a warm fire in the stove. Then, she retrieved the presents and other items from the trunk of the car and stealthily began decorating. The girls slept soundly, but whenever one turned or when Betty talked in her sleep, Hilda's heart quickened. She placed the candles around the room and decorated the "tree" with sequin-covered paper ornaments she had made. Below the "tree," she placed the presents, and stockings she had made from scraps of fabric. Each contained the beloved orange, a few nuts, and two pennies each.

She lit the candles, put milk on the stove to warm for hot chocolate, fried bacon (a rare treat), and whipped eggs for a pancake soufflé which the kids had never had before. They would love it with the sweetened chokecherry syrup simmering on the stove.

The rooster's second crow—or maybe the smell of bacon—woke Jesse. His squeals as he descended the attic ladder roused the other sleepy-eyed kids from bed.

Hilda nudged the tree—a tumbleweed she'd hung upside down—to set it spinning. In the light of the candles, it glittered and glowed as it spun from a ceiling hook. Below the tree, sparkling silhouettes danced on the floor and walls. It twinkled over the stockings, new clothes, and other gifts; a magical display.

Soon joyful shrieks filled the room. The kids flitted around in the gleaming patterns the spinning tumbleweed created.

"Mother! We've never had a hanging tree before. It's beautiful." Betty turned to hug Hilda. "I can't wait to tell my friends. They'll be so jealous."

While the soufflé finished baking, the kids tore into the stockings. They jumped up and down and cried when they saw the oranges.

Next, they attacked the stacks of presents starting with the sometimes amazing sibling gifts—especially the boat Jesse made for Paul out of bark with a stick crew and a pirate flag.

Without encouragement, each child hugged the other when they opened those homemade offerings.

In the midst of the melee, Dorothy brought out a wrapped present from under her bed and handed it to her mother. Inside the package, Hilda found a picture Dorothy had painted of the juniper-dotted hillside across the valley. Hilda thanked Dorothy and started to embrace her, but hesitated.

"This is the best worst Christmas ever," Dorothy said, opening her arms to her mother. It didn't last long, that teenage hug, but it brought tears of joy to Hilda.

"Merry Christmas my darlings."

About the Authors

Drienie Hattingh is an award-winning columnist and author. Her work has been published in newspapers and magazines in America and South Africa. She authored the historical novel,

Forever Friends, A Glass Slipper for Christmas, and The Last Gas Station. She also published four anthologies based on legends in Utah. Drienie and her husband, Johan, relocated to Gig Harbor, Washington, from Utah. They have three children and two grandchildren. Their traditional holiday celebration includes a home-cooked Christmas Eve dinner where they take turns reading a page from the Little Golden Book version of *The Christmas Story*.

Mikki Ashton is a mother of two, grandmother of five whom she makes it her mission to spoil. She works as an Instructional Designer. Her passion includes football, the outdoors, and all things shiny, which might be why she loves Christmas so much. When she was a child, Christmas was the only day she did not feel poor.

Ilze Botha was born in a very small town, Matatiehle, in the Transkei, in South Africa. She grew up in Bloemfontein, Free State, where she met her husband. They have three children. They lived in Cape Town, South Africa, before immigrating to Albuquerque, New Mexico. Ilze is a baker. They have a dog, Hannah, and a wild bunny who has claimed their backyard for himself.

Elsabe Botha owns a flower farm in the Western Cape, South Africa. She and her son, Reinhart, run the farm and harvest Proteas for export and for local florists. Her  husband, Butch works in East London as a road construction engineer. Their daughter, Roelien, an insurance agent, is married and lives in Gauteng. Elsabe loves Christmas because that is one of the few times a year when they are all together.

Celeste Canning is an attorney by day and human slave to the four-footed overlords by night. In between the two jobs, she finds time to  enjoy the beautiful place she lives, outside of Ogden, Utah, with her husband (and the four-footed overlords), read books, sew a thing or two, and cook a few meals. She has recently discovered she is the most boring person on earth and likes it. She loves Christmas - "It Rocks!"

Terry Clancy claims Kirkland, Washington, as her hometown. She grew up all over. Her heart is in Geneva, Switzerland, where she spent her formative years. She currently lives in Ogden, Utah, with her two cats, Sebastian and Coco. She has two grown children, Maureen and Ian. Christmas is Terry's favorite time of year because she feels the world is a little bit nicer during this season.

Erika De Wet grew up in South Africa. She is married with two children and lives on Long Island, New York. Her big love in life is traveling and hiking. She also loves tennis, cycling, photography, and music. One of her biggest accomplishments was walking 560 miles of the Camino de Santiago, Spain in thirty-three days. She loves the magic of Christmas, being together as family and friends in a festive atmosphere.

Barbara Emanuelson lives in Wilmington, North Carolina. She is an award-winning writer. She is the mother of three amazing daughters and the wife of a Greek Orthodox Christian priest. She loves everything about Christmas, including serving in her church choir, playing Christmas carols on her antique piano, cooking many holiday sweets from  her Hellenic heritage, and decorating her home. She's a life-long mother of feline fur babies.

Doug Gibson lives in Ogden, Utah, with his wife, Kati, and children. After a long career as a journalist, he now reviews business taxes for the Internal Revenue Service. Kati is a third-grade  teacher. He's loved Christmas ever since he and his siblings greeted the holiday at 4 a.m. His children usually allow him to sleep in until 7 a.m.

Marley Gibson is a bestselling author of over thirty books in young adult, women's fiction, contemporary romance, and non-fiction. She has always loved the Christmas season, decorations, and celebrations since her birthday falls between Christmas and New Year's. A home chef, SCUBA diver, and avid traveler, Marley and her husband, Patrick Burns, live in Savannah, Georgia, with their precious rescue cats, Madison and Boo. They also

own and operate Exploration Point Tours.

Erica Hattingh-Smith was born in South Africa and immigrated to New Zealand with her family. She is a teacher in an elementary school. She

lives in Tauranga, with her husband, Wayne. She has three children and four grandchildren with the fifth on the way. She loves Christmas because it is a time for giving and spending.

Brenda Hattingh splits her time between Salt Lake City, Duchesne, Utah and wherever the wind blows her. When she isn't painting, writing, acting or playing music, you will most likely find her on a camping or hiking adventure with her boyfriend Eric and their two dogs, Wyatt and Levon. She works part-time at the Paint Mixer, teaching people to paint and she performs as a clown at birthday parties. She also does  pet portrait commissions. Look for her Facebook page, Wy-Guy Painted Pet Portraits! She loves Christmas because it makes her slow down and takes stock of everything she is grateful for.

Alex Montanez was born in Ogden, Utah. He enjoys poetry, producing podcasts and dabbles in a little acting. He is the owner of Rovali's on  Historic 25th Street in Ogden. He is married and has two grown daughters, two sons-in-law, and two grandchildren. He loves and supports his community and Christmas to him is memories, family, and peace.

Penny Ogle has a Bachelor of Science in Business Management. She and her husband live in the Ogden Valley, in Utah. Their four children have presented them with a grand total of thirteen grandchildren. She loves being a grandma and creating memories for friends and family. If you can't find her at home, she might be at a grandchild's activity,  working, traveling, or Tap Dancing. Christmas means, 'going home' to Penny. As she unpacks her collection of Christmas ornaments, those who truly can't go home return to her heart.

Deb Rockwell of Kaysville, Utah, is a divorced mother of two, Andrea and Ryan, and has two grandbabies, Taiyden and Amberlyn. Her career as a Licensed Massage Therapist has been a joy  in her life. She believes in the "Power of Touch" to heal not only the body, but, the heart, as well. Deb loves the Christmas story and the joy the Season brings. She wishes you all a very Merry Christmas.

Rebecca Ory Hernandez lives in Ogden, Utah, with her husband and son. She enjoys writing, gardening, cooking, and painting. She works with children as a school librarian during the week. Rebecca's son's birthday is Christmas Eve, so she makes it special for him and always reads *The Cajun Night Before Christmas.* She loves the traditions of a Cajun Christmas, including the culture, food, decorating the

tree with home-made ornaments, bonfires, Mass, and family gatherings. *The Nutcracker* is also part of their Christmas tradition since her son performs in it every year.

Lizell Sillman lives in a small town in Georgia with her husband and two children. She is an

importer of Fairtrade Children's clothing and avid baker in her spare time. Christmas for the Sillman's is about celebrating Christ, family, love, and the magical wonders of children's imaginations.

Juli Robertson lives in Pretoria, South Africa. She and her husband own a Bed and Breakfast. She has three sons and a granddaughter. They get together on Christmas Eve, have a special dinner, and give each other handmade gag and other gifts. On Christmas day, they have cold meats and salads as a nod to the South African summer weather. Juli loves an afternoon thunderstorm to remind her who is in charge on Christmas day.

Margaret Zeemer was born in London, UK. She immigrated to the USA in the 1960s. She is a widow and has two adult children and one grandson. She now lives in Ogden, Utah with her Golden Retriever. Owner of the Wisebird Bookery and Grounds for Coffee, a local hangout for book lovers, she is now retired and looks forward to following her dream of writing the stories of her travels around the world. She loves Christmas because she feels something wonderful always happens in this season. There is a spirit of hope, joy, goodwill, and brotherhood and a lot of glitter, too.

Lynda West Scott lives in Santa Cruz, California where she is a Realtor.* Lynda enjoyed collaborating with Drienie Hattingh on two spooky anthologies. Oh, the stories they could tell. Eight of Lynda's short stories have been published and her articles appeared in several Utah magazines. Lynda and her husband have six (his/her) children and

eight grandkids. Christmas is a family event celebrated with traditions. *The Best Worst Christmas* was inspired by her grandmother. Watch for Lynda's novel, *Without Reason,* in 2018.

Drienie Hattingh's special memory:

My husband, Johan, with our grandsons, Tristan and Simon.

Made in the USA
Columbia, SC
23 November 2017